PERRYVILLE UNDER★FIRE

PERRYVILLE UNDER★FIRE

THE AFTERMATH OF KENTUCKY'S LARGEST CIVIL WAR BATTLE

STUART W. SANDERS

THE
History
PRESS

Published by The History Press
Charleston, SC 29403
www.historypress.net

Cover image: The 9th Indiana Infantry marching into Danville, Kentucky, following the Battle of Perryville. *From* Harper's Weekly.

First published 2012

ISBN 78-1-5402-0687-9

Library of Congress Cataloging-in-Publication Data
Sanders, Stuart W.
Perryville under fire : the aftermath of Kentucky's largest Civil War battle / Stuart W.
Sanders.
pages cm
Includes bibliographical references and index.
ISBN 78-1-5402-0687-9
1. Perryville, Battle of, Perryville, Ky., 1862. 2. Perryville, Battle of, Perryville, Ky.,
1862--Influence. 3. Perryville, Battle of, Perryville, Ky., 1862--Social aspects. 4. Perryville
(Ky.)--History--19th century. I. Title.
E474.39.S25 2012
973.7'33--dc23
2012000023

CONTENTS

ACKNOWLEDGEMENTS

O n October 8, 1862, more than 7,500 Union and Confederate troops were killed and wounded outside of Perryville, Kentucky. This battle proved to be the Bluegrass State's largest, and many veterans remarked that it was the most intense fight that they ever experienced. Nearly every barn, home, shed, stable, business, school and church became makeshift hospitals, and the burden of caring for the massive number of casualties fell upon Perryville's 300 inhabitants and the residents of other nearby communities. Union doctors were woefully unprepared for the large number of injured soldiers. A drought and lack of anesthesia accentuated the suffering, and delayed burials made the battlefield a horrific environment. The day after the fight, Henry Fales Perry of the 38th Indiana Infantry Regiment aptly described the scene. "The spectacle presented by the battlefield was enough to make angels weep," he lamented. "It beggars all description."

For nearly a decade, I was fortunate to work for the Perryville Battlefield Preservation Association, a not-for-profit organization charged with preserving and interpreting Kentucky's largest Civil War battleground. During my time there, my office was located along the town's nineteenth-century commercial district. Therefore, I had ample time to reflect on what soldiers, civilians and surgeons experienced. I also became curious about what happened to the town and region once the firing stopped. This book hopes to answer that question, and numerous friends and colleagues have helped along the way.

ACKNOWLEDGEMENTS

First, I must thank Captain Robert C. Peniston, U.S. Navy, retired, for giving me my first job in the field of Civil War history. Captain Peniston hired me as a docent at the Lee Chapel in Lexington, Virginia, when I was sixteen years old. He has been a wonderful mentor, friend and generous role model who helped lead me into the field of public history. I am thankful for his guidance and lifelong friendship.

Much appreciation goes to the board of directors of the Perryville Battlefield Preservation Association (PBPA) and the Perryville Battlefield Commission. I especially thank former board presidents Kent Masterson Brown, Don C. Kelly and Dr. Clarence Wyatt for their support during my tenure there. David L. Morgan, former executive director of the Kentucky Heritage Council, was also a mentor and friend. Alan and Arleen Hoeweler have also been incredibly generous, from allowing me to stay at the historic H.P. Bottom House when I began working in Perryville to letting my wife and me use that incredible house for our wedding reception. Special thanks also go to Darrell Young, one of the first people I met in Perryville, who has incredible insight about the battle and the aftermath. Tours of the region with him were always greatly appreciated.

I am also grateful to my friends at the Kentucky Department of Parks, the Kentucky Heritage Council and the many Kentucky Civil War sites and state agencies who generously helped me during my time in Perryville. Others include former colleagues Bobby Joe Ellis, Krista Rinehart and Jacky Thomas, Kay Berggren, Lisa Bottom, Sue Bottoms, Joe Brent, Dwight Conley, Carolyn Crabtree, John Downs, Harold Edwards, Tom Fugate, Ren Hankla, Scott Hankla, Joni House, the late Brooks Howard, Nicky Hughes, Sherry Jelsma, Mary Lynn, Mary Quinn Ramer, Bruce Richardson, Richard Stallings, Roger Stapleton, former Boyle County judge executive Tony Wilder, the late Bill Wilson and many more. After spending nearly ten years in Perryville constantly relying on myriad people and agencies, there are too many people to thank here. For those I have failed to mention, please know how I have appreciated your support and friendship.

I am now thankful and honored to still work in the public history field in the Commonwealth of Kentucky. Many thanks are especially due to my boss, Kent Whitworth. Appropriately, I first met Kent on the Perryville battlefield, and I am grateful for his encouragement, trust and support. Additional thanks go to my other colleagues, who are too numerous to mention. Please know how much I enjoy working with you.

Several friends and archivists helped with supplying illustrations. Many thanks to Andre Brousseau, Old Crow Inn (Danville); Bob Glass, Centre College; Jennifer Duplaga, Kentucky Historical Society; JoAnn Hamm, Kentucky School for the Deaf; Russ Hatter, Capital City Museum (Frankfort); Kurt Holman, Perryville Battlefield State Historic Site; Joanie Lukins; Susan Lyons Hughes, Shaker Village at Pleasant Hill; Jim Miller; Jean Kernen Moses; Elizabeth and Robert Orndorff; Bruce Richardson, Elmwood Inn (Perryville); Jerry Sampson; Reverend Jim Stewart, Presbyterian Church of Danville; and Kelli Thompson, Kentucky Historical Society.

I am also grateful for supportive friends Erik Drake and Mignon Brousseau, Brian Grimmer, Steve and Amy Isola, Andrew McNeill, John and Andrea Mesplay, Mark Read, John Walsh, Robert H. Williams and W.L. Wilson. With additional gratitude to my in-laws, Gary and Cindy Neighbors, Brian and Heather Neighbors, D.C. and Virginia Neighbors and John and Evelyn Renner. Appreciation for my brother, Wallace Sanders, and my sister-in-law, Catherine Edwards Sanders.

The generosity of Dr. Kenneth Noe, author of *Perryville: This Grand Havoc of Battle*, who donated his research files to the Perryville battlefield, greatly assisted this project. Robert Ellis, archivist at the National Archives and Records Administration in Washington, D.C., was instrumental in finding war claims pertaining to institutions that were damaged after the battle.

I am also grateful to Will McKay, my editor at The History Press, and the rest of the staff there who have helped make this project possible.

Importantly, this project would not have been possible without Kurt Holman, manager of the Perryville Battlefield State Historic Site. No one knows the Battle of Perryville as well as Kurt, and I am grateful for his expertise, his generosity with his research files and his suggestions to this manuscript. His insight has been invaluable, and I appreciate his support and friendship.

A multitude of thanks goes to my friend, colleague and fellow carpooler Don Rightmyer, who encouraged me throughout the completion of this project. Don and his wife, Bonnie, both read the manuscript and offered valuable suggestions. With many early mornings and innumerable hours spent on the road carpooling, I am appreciative of Don's encouragement and friendship, which is *ausgezeichnet*.

I am very grateful to my parents, Dr. I. Taylor Sanders II and Barbara Wilson Sanders, who have read almost every word that I have ever written. This project could not have been completed without their support, advice and encouragement. My father, who recently retired after forty-two years of teaching history at Washington and Lee University, and my mother, a former English teacher, are wonderful editors. They are, however, even better parents. Words cannot express how grateful I am to them.

I am incredibly thankful to my wife, Jenny, and my children, John, Anne and Elizabeth, for their patience, love, encouragement and support. I am grateful to have each of you in my life, and I love you more than you will ever know. For that reason, this book is dedicated to you.

Chapter 1

THE BATTLE OF
PERRYVILLE

S everal weeks after Kentucky's largest Civil War battle raged at Perryville, a small riverside village of three hundred inhabitants, a correspondent from Indiana's *New Albany Daily Ledger* expressed indignation about civilians visiting the battlefield. These visitors—many of them residents of neighboring states—were digging up corpses in order to reclaim the bodies of their loved ones who had died in the fight. The writer shuddered that "much and just complaint" was made against these civilians, for if they exhumed the wrong body, "in nearly every instance where the scantily covered graves are opened by these citizens, they are only partially filled up again." This, the scribe lamented, kept the field in a perpetual state of horror. "From this cause the remains of the dead are left exposed," he wrote; "here an arm, there a leg, and again a head with its ghastly face, from which the rotten flesh is dropping, and upon all which the hogs feed at will. The thought of such things is of itself horrible; its realization terrible in the extreme. No more civilians should be allowed to open graves upon the battle-field…such scenes of desecration upon its sacred soil are outrages which should never be tolerated."[1]

Perryville residents—and citizens of other nearby communities—contended with these horrific conditions for months after the battle. Wounded and sick soldiers filled churches and homes, confiscated livestock, consumed winter stores, burned fences and damaged schools, residences and houses of worship. When it rained, the limbs of deceased soldiers popped up from shallow graves. Many residents never recovered—economically or psychologically—from the aftermath of the Battle of Perryville. The local economy stagnated, schools closed, civilians succumbed to disease and Kentucky—relatively unscathed in the war's earliest months—experienced the severity of the conflict firsthand.

In the summer of 1862, the Union Army of the Ohio, commanded by Major General Don Carlos Buell, hoped to capture Chattanooga, Tennessee. Chattanooga was an important railroad junction and supply depot, and Southern commanders in east Tennessee needed a way to halt the Union advance. Although Rebel officers first considered fighting Buell in middle Tennessee, they soon shifted their plans. To protect Chattanooga and to recruit Kentuckians to the Southern cause, Confederate generals Braxton Bragg and Edmund Kirby Smith invaded Kentucky.[2]

Kirby Smith's army began the bluegrass invasion. Entering the commonwealth near Cumberland Gap, Smith's command rapidly marched northward, where they overwhelmed a Union force at Richmond. Continuing their advance, these Confederates captured Lexington and Frankfort. A Confederate Kentucky loomed on the horizon.[3]

Confederate Major General Edmund Kirby Smith, commander of the Army of Kentucky, hoped to wrest the Bluegrass State from Union control in the summer of 1862. Upon entering Kentucky, Smith reported, "My advance is made in the hope of permanently occupying Kentucky. It is a bold move, offering brilliant results, but will be accomplished only with hard fighting." Smith, whose army was not present at Perryville, won a victory at Richmond, Kentucky, early in the campaign. *Courtesy of the Kentucky Historical Society.*

Above: When
Confederate armies
invaded Kentucky
in the summer of
1862, Major General
Edmund Kirby Smith's
Army of Kentucky
entered the state near
the Cumberland Gap,
pictured here in 1862.
*Courtesy of the Kentucky
Historical Society.*

Right: Confederate
General Braxton
Bragg led his Army
of the Mississippi
into Kentucky in the
summer of 1862. His
campaign to hold
Kentucky ended after
the Battle of Perryville.
*Courtesy of the Kentucky
Historical Society.*

13

Encouraged by Smith's success, Confederate General Braxton Bragg moved his Army of the Mississippi into Kentucky near Glasgow. After besting a Union garrison at Munfordville, Bragg's brigades marched northward, pressing toward Louisville. Although the Confederates initially hoped to capture Louisville, General Buell rushed his troops to that city and saved it for the Union. With Louisville out of his grasp, Bragg halted his command at Bardstown.[4]

In Louisville, Buell devised plans to push the Confederates from the commonwealth. First, he reinforced his army with tens of thousands of recruits from Wisconsin, Indiana, Illinois and Ohio. To contend with Smith's army near Frankfort, Buell sent nearly twenty thousand troops to the capital as a diversion. The Union commander then deployed the majority of his command, numbering fifty-eight thousand men, toward Bardstown. These troops were to seek and destroy Bragg's army, which had withdrawn eastward from Bardstown to Perryville.

There were several reasons why the Confederates halted at this riverside hamlet of three hundred inhabitants. First, a horrible drought plagued

Owned by Perryville merchant J.A. Burton, the building now known as the Elmwood Inn was a hospital following the Battle of Perryville. The building later became a school and, in the late twentieth century, was a popular tearoom. *Courtesy of Elmwood Inn Fine Teas.*

Kentucky, and most streams and creeks were completely dry. One soldier in the 94th Ohio commented, "The season was very dry and but little water could be obtained. The suffering in consequence of this may be inferred from the fact that the Ohio soldiers gave five dollars for a canteen full of muddy water, a dollar a drink, and many drank from standing pools [of] water that the horses refused to drink." Another Federal recalled drinking "from a pond where men and mules drank fifteen feet apart. Across the pond soldiers washed their socks and feet. And at an end of the pond floated a dead mule." The fetid water led to cases of dysentery and typhoid fever, and several men died from sunstroke during the march. Since Perryville's springs and the town's Chaplin River held some water, the Confederates stopped so their troops could fill their dry canteens. Furthermore, an extensive road network ran through the town and provided the Rebels with an easy escape if they needed to continue their eastward withdrawal. Finally, the Southerners wanted to stay between the Union army and a supply depot that they had established at Camp Dick Robinson in Bryantsville, thirty miles to the east. In case they needed to retreat to Tennessee, Confederate commanders knew that they would have to protect these supplies.[5]

In the early morning hours of October 8, an advance unit of Arkansas soldiers fought a sharp skirmish west of town against advancing Union troops. The Confederates held a ridge overlooking Doctor's Creek, but the Federals shoved them back and claimed the hill and the creek's stagnant pools of water. The first shots of the Battle of Perryville had been fired.[6]

Throughout the morning, Buell's men formed on the hills outside of town. Nearly twenty thousand Union troops deployed south of the village; twenty thousand took position west of town, and nearly eighteen thousand more formed north of Perryville. Bragg, with approximately sixteen thousand troops present, had been fooled by Buell's diversion toward Frankfort. Although the Confederate commander believed that he faced a minor enemy force at Perryville, he was significantly outnumbered. When Bragg learned about the Federal troops north of town, he decided to attack. His men marched northward and deployed for battle.

At 2:00 p.m. on October 8, after a short but intense artillery duel, Bragg's Confederates, with each brigade supported by an artillery battery, advanced against Union Major General Alexander McCook's Union 1st Corps, located north of town. On the Confederate right flank, Confederate Major General Benjamin F. Cheatham's division struck the northern end of the Union line.

The Federals, who had thought that the Confederates were withdrawing northeast toward Harrodsburg, were taken by surprise.

After an attack by Confederate Brigadier General Daniel Donelson's brigade ground to a halt, Brigadier General George Maney's Rebels struck the extreme left of the Union line. Maney moved through some woods, and while attacking raw Union troops commanded by Brigadier General William Terrill, his brigade became stuck behind a split-rail fence. Colonel George C. Porter of the 6th Tennessee recalled that the Confederates "had gone but a short distance when one of the most deadly and destructive fires that can possibly be imagined was poured in their whole line by the enemy." Lieutenant William Frierson of the 27th Tennessee agreed. "During the whole time of passing through the woods the battery was playing upon us with terrible effect," Frierson reported, "but as soon as the fence was reached, in full view of the battery, such a storm of shell, grape, canister, and Minié balls was turned loose upon us as no troops scarcely ever before encountered. Large boughs were torn from the trees, the trees themselves shattered as if by lightning, and the ground plowed in deep furrows." Despite the bombardment, the Southerners shoved Terrill's brigade back, killing Union division commander Brigadier General James S. Jackson in the process.[7]

After driving the 21st Wisconsin Infantry Regiment out of a cornfield, Maney's men continued their westward attack, crossing the Benton Road and striking a narrow hill defended by Union Colonel John C. Starkweather and twelve artillery pieces. The attack, spearheaded by the 1st Tennessee Infantry, shoved Starkweather's Federals back after three assaults. Evan Davis of the 21st Wisconsin recalled, "Their bullets came like hail. I often wondered how any of us escaped with our lives." During the charge, the 9th Tennessee lost every company commander, and Lieutenant Colonel John Patterson of the 1st Tennessee was struck in the moustache by a canister round and was killed. Maney's brigade reached the top of the hill, where a hand-to-hand fight erupted among the wheels of the guns. One Union artilleryman noted that the ground literally became slippery with blood. "Such obstinate fighting I never had seen before or since," wrote Sam Watkins of the 1st Tennessee. "The guns were discharged so rapidly that it seemed the earth itself was in a volcanic uproar. The iron storm passed through our ranks, mangling and tearing men to pieces."[8]

Starkweather's men fell back to the west and took cover on another ridge, behind a stone wall. Maney's Confederates continued to batter their line, but after several hours of fighting, exhaustion had taken its toll on the Southern

The Battle of Perryville

The Battle of Perryville, as depicted by artist Henry Moesler. *Courtesy of the Kentucky Historical Society.*

troops. The 79th Pennsylvania Infantry hit Maney in the flank before the 1st Wisconsin led a counterattack that blunted Maney's assault. The fight for the Union left ended, but not before significant casualties were incurred on both sides.[9]

Bragg's attack continued with Rebel brigades striking the Union line from north to south. After Cheatham's division struck the Union left flank, two brigades in Brigadier General Patton Anderson's division hit the Federal center. Colonel Thomas Marshall Jones's brigade of Mississippi and Alabama troops crossed Doctor's Creek and trudged westward up a high hill. Upon cresting the ridge, Jones's men were struck by two infantry brigades and six cannon. Jones tried three times to reach the Federal position, which was located on an opposite hill, but his men were cut down. Jones pulled back and was replaced by Colonel John C. Brown's brigade, but Brown's attack was also halted by the obstinate Federal defense.[10]

With Jones and Brown attempting to break the Union center, Confederate Major General Simon Bolivar Buckner's division assaulted the Union right flank, located on a hill above the Henry P. Bottom house. A Southern brigade led by Brigadier General Bushrod Johnson crossed Bottom's yard and attacked the 3rd Ohio, whose right flank ended at Bottom's barn. Buckeye Colonel John Beatty noted that "the air was filled with hissing balls, shells were exploding continuously and the noise of the guns deafening." Soon, however, an artillery shell struck the barn and ignited it. According to war correspondent Alf Burnett, "Many of [the Federal] wounded had crawled into this barn for protection, but a rebel shell exploding directly among the hay set the barn on fire, and several of our poor wounded boys perished in the flames."[11]

The smoke from the burning barn and the Confederate gunfire forced the 3rd Ohio back. Replacing them on top of the hill was the 15th Kentucky (Union) Infantry Regiment. Johnson's men ran out of ammunition and withdrew, so Brigadier General Patrick Cleburne's brigade assaulted the hill. Soon, Confederate Brigadier General Daniel W. Adams, forming on Cleburne's left, joined the attack against the 15th Kentucky. When Adams's command moved forward and struck the Kentuckians' right flank, one Confederate wrote that "suddenly brass bands broke loose and filled the woods full of music."[12]

Under attack by both Cleburne's and Adams's brigades, the 15th Kentucky withdrew. As the Union right flank broke, the Union center also collapsed, and the Federals fell back to the Dixville Crossroads, the intersection of the Benton and Mackville roads. By 4:00 p.m., both flanks of the Union army had been shoved to the west. Although the Unionists established a temporary line at the Russell House, their corps commander's headquarters, the Confederates pressed the attack. Cleburne's men ran out of ammunition, and as Adams's attack also ground to a halt, fresh Southern brigades commanded by Brigadier Generals S.A.M. Wood and St. John R. Liddell moved toward the crossroads.[13]

As Union troops redeployed around the Dixville Crossroads, nearly forty thousand other Federals sat idle west and south of Perryville, just a few miles from the fighting. Reinforcements were not sent in until late in the afternoon because these Northerners could not hear the battle. Because of Perryville's rolling terrain and the wind direction, a strange atmospheric phenomenon existed where the sound of battle was literally blocked from the Union commanders west of town. Because of this "acoustic shadow," General Buell, sitting at his headquarters some three miles from the heaviest fighting, only heard scattered shots, although nearly forty thousand troops battled for supremacy of the ridges north of town. The cannon fire made windowpanes rattle ten miles away in Danville, but many members of the two Union corps south and west of town, who were only lightly engaged that day, did not know that a major battle was taking place. Finally, at 4:00 p.m., one of McCook's aides reached Buell's headquarters and informed the stunned commander that, Buell wrote, "to my astonishment…the left corps had actually been engaged in a severe battle for several hours."[14]

As McCook's flanks collapsed, Colonel Michael Gooding's brigade, which had spent the day west of town with Gilbert's corps, entered the fight.

18

Union Colonel Michael Gooding, who led a brigade near the Russell House at the end of the day, was wounded and captured. Gooding's brigade, composed of 1,423 men, lost 133 killed, 344 wounded and 58 missing, or nearly 37 percent of its total force. *Courtesy of the Perryville Battlefield State Historic Site.*

Upon reaching the Dixville Crossroads, Gooding's command fought S.A.M. Wood's soldiers as they moved past the Russell House. William Cunningham of the 59th Illinois wrote his wife that "hundreds of balls came so close to my head & face that I could feel the wind of them...Add to the musketry the whirring of solid shot, the screaming & bursting of shell...[it was] as near pandemonium as I care to get."[15]

Wood's brigade withdrew, and Liddell's Confederates nearly seized the crossroads. Night was falling, and Union and Confederate lines, fighting just a few yards away from one another, intermingled. Gooding's brigade was torn apart at the intersection, but with night falling, the Confederates declined to press the attack. Therefore, the Union troops maintained control of the Dixville Crossroads and spent the remainder of the evening moving their supplies and equipment toward the rest of their army. Once their lines of communication were secured, the Federals abandoned the intersection and pulled back to a new defensive position, a chain of hills two hundred yards northwest of the crossroads. There would be no more fighting.[16]

Colonel Starkweather's stubborn defense on the Union left and the Confederates' inability to seize the crossroads late in the day saved McCook's corps. Had Starkweather been destroyed and the intersection left open to the Confederates, the Southerners could have slipped behind McCook's right

Split-rail fences were a common feature—and obstacle—on the Perryville battlefield. After the fight, these fields would have been strewn with the dead and wounded. *Courtesy of the Perryville Battlefield State Historic Site.*

wing, thereby cutting off his command from the rest of Buell's army. Had the crossroads been seized, McCook's corps could have been annihilated. Starkweather's stand and the Confederates' inability to seize the intersection were two key events in the Battle of Perryville.

Although the Confederate army had won a tactical victory at Perryville (it pushed back both flanks of the Union 1st Corps and killed and wounded more enemy troops), the Rebels suffered a strategic defeat. The Southerners battered the Union position north of town, but nearly forty thousand Northern troops were not engaged. That night, the Confederates learned that tens of thousands of enemy troops could fight the next day. Facing these odds, Bragg withdrew ten miles away to Harrodsburg, leaving the Confederate dead, and many wounded, on the battlefield. The Rebels, disappointed over a lack of recruits, eventually left Kentucky.

The battle lasted less than five hours, and casualties were severe. Bragg's Army of the Mississippi, fighting with approximately 16,000 troops, lost 532 killed, 2,641 wounded and 228 missing. Of the 18,000 Federals engaged, 894 were killed, 2,911 were wounded and 471 were missing. Many regiments lost more than 50 percent casualties, with the Confederate 16th Tennessee losing nearly 60 percent and the 22nd Indiana Infantry more than 65 percent of their regiments. Perryville's terrain, which consists of closely packed, consecutive ridges, put the troops fighting from ridge to ridge in proximity to one another, drastically increasing the number of casualties. With roughly 7,500 casualties incurred in less than five hours, at least 1,600 men were killed or wounded during each hour of fighting. Few battles matched this intensity.[17]

The Battle of Perryville, the largest fight to occur on Kentucky soil, was a turning point in the Civil War. Never again did a Southern army attempt to hold the commonwealth for the Confederacy. With few exceptions, after 1862, the Civil War in Kentucky was limited to cavalry raids and guerrilla activity. Although President Abraham Lincoln issued a preliminary version of the Emancipation Proclamation after Confederate General Robert E. Lee failed to hold Maryland, had Bragg won a decisive victory in the state

Most of the buildings along Perryville's nineteenth-century commercial district became hospitals after the Battle of Perryville. *Courtesy of Centre College.*

and advanced into Ohio or Indiana, Lincoln may not have had the political strength necessary to issue this edict.

Since Bragg was forced to withdraw from the commonwealth, many historians, such as Edwin C. Bearss, have called Perryville "a Pyrrhic victory." Bragg's tactical victory there could not save his doomed campaign, and the Southern commander faced an overall strategic defeat. Perryville was, therefore, as historian Lowell Harrison wrote, the "high-water mark of the Confederacy in the West." Never again would a western Confederate army push so far northward, and never again would the Rebels have the chance to influence congressional elections to bring Peace Democrats to power. Had the Confederates succeeded in Kentucky and advanced into Indiana or Ohio, the course of the Civil War would have changed. It was the greatest chance for the Rebels' western armies to alter the path of the conflict, yet success slipped through their fingers.[18]

The contending forces quickly left Perryville. The Union army slowly pursued the Confederates toward Tennessee, leaving a small contingent to oversee the Perryville buildings converted into hospitals and Southern prisoners there. The burden of caring for the thousands of wounded and sick, and the horrors of burying hundreds of Rebel dead, fell on the town's three hundred inhabitants.

Chapter 2
"SUCH IS THE EFFECTS OF WAR"

Private Sam Watkins of the 1ˢᵗ Tennessee Infantry recognized that the
Battle of Perryville was one of the most intense battles of the conflict. "I
was in every battle, skirmish and march that was made by the First Tennessee
Regiment during the war," Watkins wrote, "and I do not remember of a
harder contest and more evenly fought battle than that of Perryville. If it
had been two men wrestling, it would have been called a 'dog fall.' Both sides
claim the victory—both whipped."[19]

Union Colonel James B. Fry agreed, believing that the fight "will
stand conspicuous for its severity in the history of the rebellion," while
Federal Major General Alexander McCook, commander of the shattered
1ˢᵗ Corps, called Perryville "the bloodiest battle of modern times for the
number of troops engaged on our side." Bragg noted, "For the time
engaged it was the severest and most desperately contested engagement
within my knowledge." After the battle, Union division commander
Brigadier General Lovell H. Rousseau said that he "never was in so hot a
fight. Shiloh was nothing to it." The Kentucky officer added that Perryville
was a "hell-roaring fight." Soldiers in the ranks agreed. Private Jonathan
McElderry of the 121ˢᵗ Ohio wrote, "Thare [*sic*] was men in this battle that
war [*sic*] in the battle of Shilo [*sic*] and they say it was as hard a contested
battle for the time it lasted as Shilo."[20]

The battle's intensity was well illustrated by the casualties. Of the
Confederates fighting on the northern end of the battlefield, for example,
Brigadier General Daniel Donelson's 16ᵗʰ Tennessee endured 59 percent

Private Emanuel Rudy of the 79th Pennsylvania was wounded at Perryville and died from his injury on October 12, three days after the fight. *Courtesy of the Perryville Battlefield State Historic Site.*

casualties; Brigadier General A.P. Stewart's 4th Tennessee lost 50 percent; and Brigadier General George Maney's 9th Tennessee suffered 50 percent, his 1st Tennessee lost 45 percent and his 27th Tennessee suffered 51 percent casualties. Maney's Rebels faced Colonel John Starkweather's troops. Of Starkweather's men, the 79th Pennsylvania lost 51 percent casualties, while his 1st Wisconsin lost 49 percent. Furthermore, on the same part of the field, Union Brigadier General William Terrill's brigade of raw infantry suffered an average of 22 percent casualties. Perryville's terrain contributed to these large losses, as neophyte Federal troops established defensive positions on successive hilltops. Many of these ridges were fewer than three hundred yards apart. When the Rebels attacked one hill and then another, even the most incompetent marksman, backed by the massed fire of his comrades, could aim at the attacking Confederates and hit someone.[21]

The severity of the Battle of Perryville was enhanced by Confederate tactics, the terrain and Rebel armaments. In *Attack and Die*, authors Grady McWhiney and Perry Jamieson note that during the first three years of the war, Southern armies took the offensive in 70 percent of the major engagements, including Perryville. In most instances, the attacking Confederates suffered more casualties than the defending Unionists. Perryville was an exception, caused by inexperienced Federal defenders being caught by surprise. Furthermore, although the Northerners established defensive positions on successive hilltops, Perryville's rolling terrain allowed the charging Confederates to quickly strike one Federal position and then another, giving the reeling Unionists little time to recover. The terrain also negated some Federal artillery. Union surgeon J.G. Hatchitt remarked, "This battle was fought at very short range. The unevenness of the ground enabled the enemy to mass his troops in the hollows and ravines, and frequently threw them within a few yards of our batteries before they would be in range of our fire." Hatchitt added that the Confederates' use of "buck and ball" rounds, consisting of one large musket ball and three smaller pieces of buckshot, added to the large number of Union casualties.[22]

A comparison to more recent battles involving American troops illustrates how Perryville involved a large number of casualties in a short period of time. During the Second World War, the Pacific island battle of Tarawa was judged to be one of the U.S. Marines' hardest-fought battles. In this fight, the marines suffered 4,400 casualties in seventy-two hours. When GIs stormed the beaches during the Normandy invasion, the Americans sustained approximately 6,500 casualties. Therefore, the nearly 8,000 casualties brought down by musketry and nineteenth-century artillery in less than five hours at Perryville is staggering, indeed.[23]

Research conducted by Kurt Holman, manager of the Perryville Battlefield State Historic Site, details that the average age of soldiers killed or wounded at Perryville was twenty-five years old (out of a sample of 1,182 men). The oldest soldier was seventy years old, and the youngest was fifteen. The troops were from Alabama, Arkansas, Florida, Georgia, Illinois, Indiana, Kentucky, Louisiana, Michigan, Minnesota, Missouri, Mississippi, Ohio, Pennsylvania, Tennessee, Texas and Wisconsin. In addition, Confederate States Regulars and United States Regulars were also killed and injured. Sadly, of the more than 5,400 killed and wounded identified by Holman's research, only 633 graves have been identified.[24]

Thousands of soldiers were wounded at Perryville, and all suffered a variety of injuries. Casualties from the 41st Mississippi, which fought against the Union center, provide a good example of wounds experienced by soldiers. With 427 men engaged at Perryville, this regiment lost 21 killed and 69 wounded, or nearly 20 percent of the command. Their brigade, which included two Florida infantry regiments and a Georgia artillery battery, was commanded by Brigadier General John C. Brown, who was slightly wounded in the thigh. Their immediate commander, Colonel William F. Tucker, was severely injured in the right arm. Two lieutenants were also wounded. One, M.L.

Marshall, had his "left arm shattered, and amputated," while T.S. Slaughter died from an injury to the lungs. The *Atlanta Southern Confederacy* detailed these casualties, and one can imagine—as in *Gone With the Wind*—civilians poring over the pages to discover the fates of their loved ones. Casualties in the 41st Mississippi included George Deere, who was wounded in the right side of his chest and had his right arm broken. In addition, R.D. Ford had his "right arm shattered and amputated"; A.J. Payne was shot in the hip and the "ball not extracted"; F.G. Rowe was hit in both the left arm and his right thigh; and C.G. Stanford was shot in the lung and died. W.P. Ware was shot "in shoulder, ball lodged in neck," while M. Freeman had his "right arm shattered" and amputated. All of the injuries listed appear to be musket wounds, except for that of J.R. Hunt, who was wounded in the shoulder by "a shell."[25]

When night fell and the battle ended, an informal truce fell over the field as troops searched for wounded comrades by torchlight. Federal Captain Robert Taylor helped remove the injured from the battlefield. He recalled that shortly after the firing stopped, "we started upon our mournful mission.

Union Captain Robert Taylor, shown here in a postwar photograph, removed wounded soldiers from the battlefield after the fight. *Courtesy of Jean Kernen Moses.*

There were already five or six parties of the character on the field and every step we made toward the front we met an ambulance returning slowly from the late scene of action, with its groaning brethren." While many wounded were taken from the battlefield that night, some injured were removed more than five days after the fight. These forgotten troops had yet to receive any medical attention. By mid-October, more than 2,500 Union and Confederate wounded filled Perryville's makeshift hospitals, including 1,745 Federal troops and 905 Rebel soldiers. Most of the wounded Southerners were transported to Harrodsburg during Bragg's retreat.[26]

Although night had fallen, the field was still dangerous. Captain Edward Bowers, a chaplain in the 105th Ohio Infantry, held a prayer service near the northern end of the battlefield. These survivors had much to be thankful for. The inexperienced regiment was hit hard by Confederate General George Maney's brigade and lost nearly 32 percent casualties. Upon hearing a hymn, the regiment's colonel ordered the clergyman to stop the singing in case it drew enemy fire. The somber tune could have escaped Rebel volleys, for most stretcher-bearers and battlefield searchers left their weapons in camp in order to temper any hostility.[27]

Although most battlefield searchers were unarmed, some sporadic firing continued at dusk. When a member of the 41st Georgia walked across the field, he was struck in the right cheek by a spent musket ball. The shot knocked the soldier down and gave him a black eye that lasted for several weeks. Some Unionists were crack shots, and this Georgian was fortunate that the injury was not more severe.[28]

At least one soldier took advantage of this informal truce to get out of the war. Sergeant John Dey of the 21st Wisconsin Infantry informed his superiors that he had been captured and paroled by Southern troops while searching for the wounded. Dey slipped off to Louisville to await exchange, but several of Dey's comrades later informed regimental officers that the sergeant had approached an unarmed group of Confederates who had warned him that he would be "taken" if he neared them. Despite the warning, Dey approached the Southerners, engaged in a "low conversation," handed over his sword and secured a parole. Federal authorities hoped to court-martial Dey, Sergeant John Otto of the 21st Wisconsin wrote, because it was "a clear case of desertion under aggravating circumstances." Many were shocked by the behavior of this forty-year-old man, who was a prominent member of his community. Otto concluded, "Perhaps Sergeant Dey lost his patriotism there in the cornfield [where the regiment had been decimated], or on the retreat and concluded to let the other boys do the fighting." Dey reported to a parole camp in Dayton, Ohio, and was exchanged in December 1862. Ordered back to his company, no one was surprised when Dey failed to appear. For this Wisconsin soldier, older than most in his unit, one battle was enough.[29]

Despite some continued violence and the taking of prisoners, compassion did exist between enemy soldiers. One instance occurred after Corporal Will Woodward of the 79th Pennsylvania Infantry was wounded in the left side by a buck and ball round. The musket ball struck him between his left nipple and sternum before exiting near his shoulder blade. Two pieces of shot struck his lungs, and Woodward also lost a finger and part of his ear. After lying on the battlefield for more than ten hours, "an unlikely savior" arrived. A soldier from the 41st Georgia stumbled upon the injured Pennsylvanian, saw that his canteen was empty and gave him some water. Despite the drought and Woodward's apparently fatal wounds, the Southerner traded his full wooden canteen with Woodward's empty one. The Georgian said that he had purchased the canteen in Atlanta when he left for the war. Before departing, he told Woodward that "he had carried the canteen in many battles and survived." It proved to be a good token. Woodward lived through the war.[30]

Compassion was reciprocated. As night fell, Captain B.P. Steele of the 1st Tennessee lay severely wounded on the crest of a hill that his regiment had attacked. A captain from the 1st Wisconsin found Steele, "expressed his sorrow at the Confederate's condition, moved him into a comfortable position, and gave him water from a canteen." Hours before, the two enemy regiments had struggled for supremacy of the ridge. In 1904, Steele searched for the generous officer through a notice in *Confederate Veteran* magazine. Another soldier wrote that Steele "never recovered fully from the wounds, but for nearly half a century suffered cheerfully."[31]

The informal truce allowed the Southerners to prepare for further campaigning. With arms and accoutrements scattered across the battlefield, Confederates replenished their weapons and tattered uniforms. Maney's artillery chief, Captain William Turner, traded his two six-pounder guns for two Federal Napoleons and filled his caissons with captured ammunition. Captain William Carnes's battery, which fired on the Union left from the northernmost Confederate position, also traded its damaged guns for captured Federal pieces. Furthermore, division commander Major General Benjamin F. Cheatham noted, "Every man of my command brought from the battle-field [the] next morning two guns (muskets) each, hoping to find transportation to haul them off with me. As our wounded filled all of our extra wagons, they were left on the ground in a line the length of the command."[32]

Federal officers who later found the discarded guns questioned why so many rifles were neatly lined up near the battlefield. "At one point," Union Colonel William Carlin pondered, "we marched by a line of muskets lying on the ground in a straight line, as if the troops (Confederate) to which they belonged had formally thrown them down to an enemy. How they happened to be abandoned there I never learned." Another soldier, William H. Ball of the 5th Wisconsin Artillery, was also perplexed by the weapons yet gave Union gunners credit. He wrote, "I saw a good many hundred muskets thrown down in line and left by a regiment or brigade of rebels, who must have become panic-stricken by our cannonading and fled." A newspaper correspondent related that "enough guns, most of them loaded, were found down the rear of the spring, to arm two or three regiments."[33]

In addition to grabbing guns, the Confederates also replaced their worn uniforms. One of Donelson's men stated, "We got a lot of good, warm blankets and comfortable blue suits in this fight." Later, Federal troops refused to bury Southern corpses because the secessionists had stripped Northern bodies. An angry correspondent from the *Cincinnati Daily Enquirer* reported:

> *Roving parties from both armies wandered over the battle-field, most of which was held by the enemy—some to look after missing friends, but more to rifle and outrage the dead...a survey of the field displayed the disgusting sight of all the dead, denuded of coats, hats, pants and shoes, and all the pockets left turned inside out. Undoubtedly most of this was done by the rebels, for the clothes they exchanged for those they had stolen, left on the field, told the tale.*[34]

One corpse that was stripped was that of Captain Charles Olmstead of Company A, 42nd Indiana Infantry. During the battle, the 42nd Indiana had been ordered to charge the Rebels as they attacked the center of the Union line. Advancing, Olmstead shouted, "Come on, boys!" As he yelled, "This is as good a place to die as any other," he was shot in the forehead and killed. When the bullet struck, Olmstead's brains splattered over George Kirkpatrick and another soldier. Olmstead was one of the favorite officers in the regiment, and the thirty-eight-year-old captain was survived by a wife and four children. On the morning after the fight, six Hoosiers returned

Private Henry Hunter, 42nd Indiana Infantry Regiment, was killed in action. His brother, Reuben Hunter, part of the same regiment, was wounded. *Courtesy of the Perryville Battlefield State Historic Site.*

Private Reuben Hunter, 42nd Indiana Infantry Regiment, was wounded at Perryville, while his brother, Henry, was killed. *Courtesy of the Perryville Battlefield State Historic Site.*

to bury the officer. These men discovered that the Rebels had taken all of Olmstead's clothing, except for his shoes and underwear.[35]

Although some plundered, most of the troops were on the field to remove the wounded and slain. A member of Cheatham's division, Major J.T.

Williamson of the 51st Tennessee, clearly remembered the suffering. He wrote that Perryville "was the hottest fight for the time it lasted that I was in during the war. We slept right on the ground where we had made the last charge. The dead Yankees were lying thick on the ground." He added, "A pathetic scene took place that night. A Federal soldier boy was wounded and lying near where we were bivouacked. He begged piteously for his mother and to be taken away as [he feared that] the fight would be renewed the next day."[36]

Corporal James Crawford of the 80th Illinois also looked for dead and wounded comrades. "After the fight I went over the battleground," he recalled. "And Oh what a sight, the dead, the dying, and the wounded. Some with there [sic] legs or arms shot off, some lying dead on the field. I seen [sic] the body of John Wilson lying on the field. He was an Uncle to the Huddleson boys. It went very hard on them to see him lying dead, but such is the effects of war."[37]

The aftermath was particularly shocking to neophyte soldiers. Mead Holmes of the 21st Wisconsin was ordered to find water and missed his regiment's slaughter. When he returned that night, he removed the dead and injured. "The moon shone full upon the scene," Holmes detailed. "It is utterly useless to describe the sight—men and horses dead and wounded, wagon-wheels, arms, caissons scattered, and the moans and shrieks of the wounded. Oh, may you never see such a sight! I helped carry off one poor fellow with his mouth and lower jaw shot off."[38]

Chapter 3
"LONG HOURS OF UNNOTED AGONY"

The battleground presented terrible scenes for those who toured the area. "The road for miles was strewn with clothing, muskets, and military trappings of every description," a member of the 36th Illinois Infantry Regiment wrote. "Every farm house and barn along the route was tenanted with wounded rebels...some of them with hardly life enough remaining to realize the horrors of their situation; others mangled and bleeding, presented sad sights and sounds, never to be forgotten." A Hoosier soldier concurred, remarking, "Upon visiting the battle field [the] next day a sad sight was presented to view. The dead...lay just as they had fallen. Some with features calm and serene, others ghastly and distorted, some mangled and torn, others pierced by a single ball."[39]

The battle was a great equalizer, with enlisted men and officers meeting the same fate. At dawn on October 9, Union Captain Samuel Starling looked for the corpse of his commander, Brigadier General James S. Jackson. Near the hill where Jackson had been slain, Starling "found quite a number of Rebel and Union soldiers, ministering to the wounded and looking at the ground." Between these foes, Starling recalled, "all animosity had ceased and they were mixing like friends." The officer found Jackson's body, but the general's boots, hat and buttons were gone.[40]

War correspondents also investigated the battleground. A reporter from the *Louisville Journal* eyed a hill on the Union left flank that Union Colonel John C. Starkweather's men had defended. The correspondent noted the effectiveness of Federal artillery. "I this morning saw four dead rebels who had been killed by a single shot," the reporter wrote. "The top of the head of the first was taken off, the entire head of the second was gone, the breast of the third was torn open, and the ball passed through the abdomen of the [fourth]. All had fallen in a heap, killed instantly." These four corpses intrigued many witnesses and became a primary battlefield curiosity.[41]

Other citizens, including twelve-year-old William Caldwell McChord, who lived ten miles away in Springfield, joined the soldiers and reporters. McChord rode to Perryville to catch a glimpse of "real war." The boy rode across the initial Union lines from north to south, and what he witnessed changed his life. He wrote:

> At this point, crossing a space a quarter of a mile wide, the Federal dead were so thick that we could not ride across the battlefield without our horses stepping on the dead bodies as they were strown [sic] promiscuously on the ground. One Federal officer was shot and fell in a fence corner which was overgrown with bushes. This poor fellow was still alive but desperately wounded. I can never forget the terrible exclamations and manifestations of intense suffering when it was attempted to remove him to the field hospital. This is one of the many instances of that terrible war.[42]

Curiosity drew other local residents to the field. Robert Patterson, a mathematics professor at nearby Centre College in Danville, visited the scene thirty-six hours after the fight. His wife, Elizabeth, recorded what he witnessed. "The Confederate dead were still unburied and a shocking sight they were, with their mutilated, swollen bodies," Elizabeth wrote. "Hundreds of muskets were scattered over the field or had been gathered into heaps. Musket and cannon balls, grape, canister and shell, or fragments of shells, might be picked up on profusion in certain localities. In one place eighteen dead bodies had been gathered together by the Confederates themselves and surrounded with a fence-rail, to protect them from the hogs." Patterson's husband also found the four dead Rebels killed by artillery in front of Starkweather's position. Elizabeth explained that "in one spot four bodies were lying, said to have been killed by a single shot. Here was a poor creature with a portion of his skull carried away; there lay one with his arm torn from his body. Many had been wounded by musket balls in the head; some in the region of the heart or lungs. A few had perished instantly, it seemed, unconscious of the strike that destroyed them; while in others life must have oozed out with the heart's slow ebbing tide in long hours of unnoted agony."[43]

"Long Hours of Unnoted Agony"

Many Union soldiers were surprised that the fighting did not renew the next day. "We were expecting a big fight today, but when daylight came the rebels were retreating," penned a perplexed member of the 80th Illinois. "I then went over the battleground and there I saw the dead and wounded lying thick. They were shot in all conceivable ways and places. It was a sickening sight to see the poor fellows a lying." Bliss Morse of the 105th Ohio was also shocked. "It is a sad sight to see dead men lay with balls shot through their heads, some with arms, legs and bowels torn off," Morse wrote. "Some lay with their tongues swelled out of their mouths, and others laid with hands stuck out as if surprised, with an expression of amusement on their faces. They were very much distorted."[44]

Another Illinois soldier, Lieutenant Chesley Mosman of the 59th Illinois, wandered to the Dixville Crossroads, the intersection of the Benton and Mackville roads. Here, where Mosman's brigade had been shattered, the battle ended. The soldier wrote that around the intersection "there were not ten square feet of ground on which there were not one and sometimes two or three dead men lying." Mosman encountered another lieutenant from his regiment, John B. Adams, who had been shot in the hip. Mosman procured some water for his friend, but Adams died shortly thereafter. Several hours later, another member of the regiment found the corpse of their surgeon. The doctor had been shot in the neck and killed while dressing a soldier's wound. When his body was discovered, the surgeon's boots, watch, hat, money and surgical instruments were gone, presumably taken by the Confederates who took over the intersection after the battle.[45]

Some members of the 59th Illinois, however, were more fortunate. Lieutenant Samuel West, adjutant of the regiment, was wounded four times during the battle and continued to fight. His fifth wound, which occurred near the intersection, forced him to leave the unit. According to his brigade commander, Colonel Michael Gooding, West "did not quit the field until entirely disabled." Amazingly, West survived the battle and the squalid field hospitals. His final wound resulted in the loss of an eye, but he was fortunate to have lived.[46]

Perryville physician Dr. Jefferson J. Polk, who wandered to the battlefield from his home in downtown Perryville, recorded the disorder left by the clashing armies. Polk wrote that he

> *saw on either hand dead men and dead horses, canteens, muskets, cartridge-boxes, broken ambulances, coats, hats, and shoes, scattered thick over the*

ground...All around lay dead bodies of the soldiers...The whole scene beggars description. The ground was strewn with soiled and torn clothes, muskets, blankets, and the various accouterments of the dead soldiers. Trees not more than one foot in diameter contained from twenty to thirty musket-balls and buck-shot, put into them during the battle.[47]

George Landrum of the 2nd Ohio rode across the lines the day after the fight. "I will not attempt to describe the horrible scenes I there witnessed—men with their heads shot off, and mangled in every possible manner," Landrum wrote. "[N]o one can describe the scenes of that field. I saw a Rebel officer who had fallen on a fence that was burning, half charred."[48]

Clergymen in the ranks were also repelled by what they witnessed. W.H. Honnell, the chaplain of the 1st Kentucky Union Cavalry, passed a field hospital after the fight. "As we passed a house used by the Surgeons as an amputating hospital," he wrote, "just beyond, we could see a heap of bleeding limbs like a mound of clay, as they were cut off and thrown from the window above." Another Federal chaplain simply commented, "The battle-field is a terrible sight."[49]

In addition to witnessing amputations, the unburied bodies shocked witnesses. A Union cavalryman who rode through the area two days after the fight reported:

On Oct. 11, we reached Perryville, and marched over the battlefield. It was a sickening sight. Our dead were all buried; but the blackened corpses of rebel dead, mangled in every way possible, were still scattered over the field. It would be impossible for me to say how many were killed, but the number was enormous in proportion to the numbers engaged. I saw them lying in pens, from 8 to 19 each...I have no doubt that many are still unburied, and some have been eaten up by hogs, leaving nothing but the whitened bones to show that a fellow-creature lost his life in a war created by ambitious politicians to lengthen out their time of holding the public purse strings.

As late as October 16, more than a week after the battle, another Union officer complained, "There are hundreds of men being eaten by the buzzards and hogs." Finally, Federal authorities in Perryville impressed slaves and ordered local Southern sympathizers to bury the dead Confederates. Most of the bodies were placed into two large pits. This mass grave is now located at the Perryville Battlefield State Historic Site.[50]

"Long Hours of Unnoted Agony"

Rules of nineteenth-century warfare were also highlighted during the aftermath. The day after the battle, Major General Alexander McCook, commander of the Federal 1st Corps; Brigadier General Lovell H. Rousseau, leader of McCook's 3rd Division; and Captain Cyrus Loomis of the 1st Battery of the Michigan Light Artillery inspected the carnage. While pausing at a makeshift pen containing the remains of 17 dead Confederates, 2 Union soldiers brought in a tall enemy soldier whom the staff recognized as a Rebel captured during the fight. This Southerner had been paroled to go to Louisville and then Vicksburg for exchange. He had been caught, however, trying to slip past Federal pickets to rejoin Bragg's army near Harrodsburg. The Confederate called his parole illegal and invalid and said he was justified in attempting to escape through the lines. McCook ignored the Confederate's excuse and "condemned him to be shot, and notified him that he had but fifteen minutes to live. The man turned pale for a moment and pleaded his right, under the circumstance of his parole, to escape if he could, but in vain. General McCook was inexorable, and warned him that he had but fifteen minutes to live." The Rebel, resigned to his fate, climbed into the pen with his dead comrades, knelt and prayed that his executioners be forgiven. He stood and faced a Northern firing squad. Shots rang out, and his lifeless body collapsed into the pen. One of the officers who had, up to that point, counted 265 dead Confederates, stated, "That makes two hundred and sixty-six, my boy."[51]

Shortly thereafter, McCook, Rousseau, Loomis and several staff members encountered the group of dead soldiers from the 1st Tennessee killed by the single artillery shot. One of the staff members wrote:

> *Three of these unfortunate beings had been killed by a single cannon ball from a battery which had evidently enfiladed the line of which they formed a part. The ball in descending had taken off the top of the head of the first, leaving his features perfect in every respect, but as it was described at the time, "fairly and cleanly scooping out his brains." The second had been struck square in the face, and the only part of his features remaining was the lower jaw. The third had been struck in the breast. Each had died instantly, and they had fallen in a heap together. There was but one commentary made on this spectacle. It was uttered by the grim old artillery[man] Loomis, "what a magnificent shot."[52]*

The party also reputedly found a wounded female Confederate soldier who fought while disguised as a man. According to the staff officer, she and her husband had joined an Alabama regiment commanded by Confederate Brigadier General S.A.M. Wood. The Union officers procured a stretcher and sent her to the Russell House, a field hospital that had been McCook's headquarters. The husband later found his wounded wife, and the two eventually settled in New York.[53]

Battlefield searchers and the wounded were most concerned about hogs that roamed the field. Before the Confederates left Perryville, they hastily built pens to protect their comrades' corpses from farm animals. Many of the soldiers, likely fearing that their bodies could someday share the same fate, vividly recalled these pens. Mead Holmes noted, "We passed a cornfield of eight acres almost covered with pens made of rails and covered with straw. These are filled with dead rebels." Morse added, "Unless something is done, the country is uninhabitable...The country here is completely ruined for the present." One Hoosier simply said, "The smell from the battlefield was awful as we hurried past it."[54]

The piled fence rails were not enough to protect the dead from the free-ranging hogs that rooted up shallow graves and ate unburied bodies. Henry Fales Perry of the 38th Indiana recalled that "in several places the rebels had piled their dead like cordwood, and enclosed them in pens made of fence rails, but most of them were scattered over the field, and in many places commingled with the dead and dying of the Union Army." Charles Francis of the 88th Illinois Infantry was appalled when he saw several dead Confederates surrounded by rails. This was done, Francis remarked, "so as to protect the remains from being attacked by the swine that prowled in the woods. The disgusting sight of these animals feeding upon human gore was more than sufficient to give them immunity from sacrifice by the hungry of our army. No one could be found sufficiently hardy to talk of eating of the flesh of hogs captured near the battlefield. No! No more than if we were an army of Hebrews." It was also said that many of the hogs died after eating the human remains.[55]

There were not enough pens to protect all the bodies. The day after the fight, a member of Rousseau's staff commented that the swine "now held possession of the field." Seven days later, another Union officer informed his wife that the battleground was "the most horrid sight that ever man beheld. Today there are hundreds of men being eaten up by the buzzards and hogs." A member of the 81st Indiana told the *New Albany Daily Ledger*, "In one place lay a wounded rebel too helpless to move, and near him lay one of his dead comrades, with the top of his head torn off, and hogs eating his body—the wounded men unable to drive them away."[56]

"Long Hours of Unnoted Agony"

During the Civil War, the town of Perryville had about three hundred residents. After the battle, most of these buildings became makeshift hospitals for the thousands of wounded soldiers. *Courtesy Perryville Battlefield Preservation Association.*

Perryville's three hundred inhabitants, and the residents of other nearby communities, were left to bury the dead, feed the wounded and repair their farms after months of post-battle occupation. Nearly every inhabitant was affected. Residents' clothes were shredded for bandages, food and livestock were devoured and fences, outbuildings and furniture were burned for firewood. Homes, businesses, hotels, churches, stables, barns, sheds and taverns became field hospitals for the thousands of wounded and sick. As Union soldier Wilbur F. Hinman explained, "Nearly all the inhabitants, men, women and children, had taken to the woods in dismay when the battle began." Residents returned to find their homes and shops full of wounded troops and their winter stores consumed.[57]

Thirst, hunger, fear, property damage, the danger of catching soldiers' illnesses and the forced participation in burials were all factors that made the residents' return a harrowing experience. Furthermore, for months their homes were crowded with the ill and injured, and like the soldiers, they were horrified by what they witnessed in their community after Kentucky's largest battle.

Chapter 4
"EVERY HOUSE WAS A HOSPITAL"

uildings in Perryville and the surrounding countryside were packed with
wounded and sick soldiers. Dr. A.N. Read of the United States Sanitary
Commission (an organization much like the Red Cross) noted that as he
traveled the ten miles from Mackville to Perryville, "nearly every house was a
hospital." In Mackville, Read recalled, a sixteen-room tavern contained 150
wounded and 30 sick soldiers. Of these, 25 were on cots, while the others lay
on the cold, straw-covered floor.[58]

Conditions in Perryville were just as Spartan. One Federal surgeon
remarked, "All the buildings suitable for the purpose that could be obtained
in the district were immediately taken for hospitals." He further noted,
"Those [wounded] belonging to the rebels were found scattered through
the neighboring woods, and in such houses, barns and stables as could be
obtained during the hasty retreat of their army." Another doctor wrote that
in Perryville, "Every house was a hospital, all crowded, with very little to
eat." Union soldier William T. Clark simply commented, "The dead and
dying are in every house."[59]

On October 9, Wilbur Hinman of the 6th Ohio Artillery, which had
spent the battle south of town with Major General Thomas L. Crittenden's
corps, traveled northward. "We moved through the little town of Perryville,"
Hinman wrote. "The village was full of the wounded of both armies. Every
house was a hospital...Part of the fighting was very near the town, and many
of the houses were riddled with shot and bullets." The Buckeye artilleryman
added, "All around us were evidences of the death struggle the day before.

Bodies of men and horses lay scattered about, in the fields and by the roadside. Every house and barn was filled with the maimed, the dying, and the dead."[60]

On October 13, the *Louisville Journal* reported similar conditions. "Perryville is entirely exhausted of provisions," a correspondent wrote, "and all the houses and churches are riddled by the fire of artillery." A member of the 1st Ohio Artillery commented that the town "presented the appearance of hard usage from the effects of the battle…Nearly every house was more or less riddled by shot and shell."[61]

Grisly conditions greeted all who visited the town. When war correspondent Alf Burnett entered the Perryville Methodist Church, he found that "the boys of the 10th and 3rd Ohio were crowded into a little church, each pew answering for a private apartment for a wounded man… [One] boy of the 10th had his entire right cheek cut off by a piece of a shell, lacerating his tongue in the most horrible manner." Circumstances were similar all over Perryville. At the Perryville seminary, which was likely a school known as Harmonia College on the east end of the village, seventy-nine severely wounded soldiers were crammed into five rooms.[62]

At these hospitals, there were few surgeons and, subsequently, little medical attention for the injured. Private Michael Hazzard of the 38th Indiana Infantry was "shot through the right shoulder, the ball passing through the lower edge of the shoulder blade. It was seven days before his bloody clothes were removed and proper surgical attention given him." Many soldiers at Perryville had similar experiences.[63]

L.W. Day of the 101st Ohio Infantry described a typical Perryville field hospital. Day wrote that he marched by

> *an old house used as a general hospital. We had never seen such a sight before. Surgeons of both armies were very busy, the evidence of their efforts being visible on every hand. Doubtless they were kind-hearted and careful, but to us it seemed like brutality. There were several piles of amputated limbs, to which accessions were being made constantly. Dead and dying men were lying promiscuously around. Others were awaiting their turn to be thrown upon the operating table, an old work bench, while still others were being bandaged and patched up in various ways and assigned to this hospital or that as the character of the injury might indicate. Some seemed to be resigned, others were cross and snappy. Some prayed, some cursed.*[64]

"Every House Was a Hospital"

David B. Griffin, a soldier in the 2nd Minnesota Infantry who was killed less than a year later at the Battle of Chickamauga, wandered into a Confederate hospital. Griffin noted that "it was a sight to behold. They were amputating legs and arms on all sides. Some were dying; others dying and calling upon absent friends and praying to die. It was a sight that I hope I may never see again."[65]

Local doctors aided the wounded at these hospitals. One of them, Perryville resident Dr. Jefferson J. Polk, who moonlighted as a minister and temperance crusader, bore the sufferings with stoicism. Polk left retirement to help the wounded, and eight to ten injured convalesced in his home. Several, including a Confederate surgeon who was taken ill, died there. In addition, Polk was appointed surgeon to a hospital that contained forty wounded troops. According to local legend, the hospital was a barn located near the battlefield. As Polk operated, the tale holds, the farmer who owned the barn played his fiddle in tune to the cries of the wounded. Sarah Coleman of

This cabin on the Perryville battlefield, from a photograph taken in 1885, was likely a makeshift hospital. Wounded men would have been crammed inside, under the tree and in the fields around this structure. *Courtesy of the Perryville Battlefield State Historic Site.*

Maxville, Wisconsin, encountered the doctor when she traveled to Kentucky to find her wounded brother. After a long journey to Perryville, she stayed in Polk's home. She remarked, "The hotels were [crowded], and every house seemed to be a hospital. [Polk] had several of the wounded at his house."[66]

Because many of the Union soldiers who fought at Perryville were from states immediately north of Kentucky, the location of the battle gave wounded troops' family members the opportunity to travel to the battlefield to try to find their injured relatives. As the largest battle to take place in proximity to Ohio, Indiana, Illinois and Wisconsin, some soldiers' families became intimately involved with the aftermath of the struggle. In addition, having these relatives visit the Perryville hospitals and the battlefield to dig up graves to look for family members spread the effect of the aftermath into neighboring states, thereby greatly expanding the impact of Kentucky's largest battle.

Sarah Coleman's experiences well define what some of these family members endured. Her wounded brother, Charles, served in Company D of the 10th Wisconsin Infantry. Three weeks after the fight, the family learned from a newspaper that Charles had been "seriously, and perhaps fatally wounded in the head" at Perryville. With her brother's fate unknown, Sarah traveled to Kentucky to find him. Upon reaching Louisville, she found one of Charles's wounded friends, who tried to assure her that her brother was fine. He and others urged her to stay away from Perryville. Sarah, however, pressed on. After taking a train to Lebanon, she rode the twenty miles to the battlefield in an army wagon.[67]

Stopping in New Market for the night, Sarah found some members of Charles's regiment, who told her "that Charles was lying in the hospital at Perryville dangerously wounded." Sarah immediately found another ride and rushed to the village. "I shall never forget the sickening sight which met our view as we went from tent to tent among the sick and wounded," she recalled. Sarah soon learned that Charles had been found three days after the battle "on the floor of an old tin shop. The door was off its hinges and seemed to have been thrown over him." Her comatose brother was placed under the care of Dr. Polk, who lived on Perryville's main street.[68]

Since Charles "lay in a stupor" after being hit in the forehead by a spent bullet, Polk decided to operate. Before the procedure, however, Charles woke up, left Polk's home and disappeared. When Sarah found Polk, the doctor and his two daughters invited her to stay in their home. Finally, Sarah located her brother, who was under guard because he was "somewhat deranged."

She took him to a hotel and dressed his wound. "I shall never forget the feeling that came over me as I looked upon him," she wrote. "He had a soiled bandage around his head, his hair was matted with blood, and his clothes down the side were saturated with it." She noted that "he seemed so different from his former self that I could hardly keep back the tears."[69]

Sarah tried to take Charles home, but army officials sent him to a hospital in New Albany, Indiana, across the Ohio River from Louisville. There, Charles again fell into a three-day coma. The bureaucracy of military authorities prevented Charles from going home, arguing that he simply had "a mere fissure of the brain." Eventually, however, Charles received a twenty-two-day furlough and returned to Wisconsin. If Sarah had not taken Charles away from Perryville, where there were scant resources and few doctors for the hospitals, it is likely that Charles would have died.[70]

Many residents' homes were commandeered as hospitals or for other purposes. Union doctors boarded with the Karrick family for more than six

The John C. Russell house served as Union Major General Alexander McCook's headquarters during the Battle of Perryville. After the fight, it was a makeshift hospital for seventeen days. *Courtesy of the Perryville Battlefield State Historic Site.*

months, and John C. Russell's residence served as a hospital for seventeen days. Because of the occupation, Russell lost thirty cords of wood, forty barrels of corn, two thousand bundles of sheaf wheat, one thousand pounds of hay and four horses. One witness noted that Russell's "house was used as a hospital and everything about it used and destroyed." The loss for these items was $845.60, which the U.S. government never repaid.[71]

Because of the chaos and uncertainty immediately after the battle, most of the field hospitals were haphazardly arranged, with soldiers setting up aid stations wherever they could find shelter. Union soldier S.K. Crawford wrote that since the Federal medical department was "poorly organized," regimental surgeons chose their own hospitals "to which their wounded might be immediately removed, and as the lines were shifting, places of safety for such depots were selected with difficulty." An angry correspondent from the *Cincinnati Daily Enquirer* condemned the lack of planning, writing that "such was the bungling of the surgical department of our army that wounded men, who could walk from the field, could not find a surgeon during the night, and all the badly wounded, whose comrades could not take them to the hospital, remained on the field until late [the next] day." The reporter would have been irate to learn that some of the injured were hauled off the battlefield more than five days after the fight.[72]

Sergeant John H. Otto of the 21st Wisconsin remembered these hastily organized hospitals. He wrote:

Our brigade was moved back now ¼ of a mile and regimental details made to look after the wounded and bring them to the hospital. That sounds very big but one must not expect [too] much of a hospital behind a battlefield. In this case the hospitals consisted of a few small houses in Perryville, two small log barns in the rear of the battlefield and one big hospital tent. The barn nearest to the line was used as an amputation room; that is [where] arms and legs were sawed off. The boys called it the "butchershop" or "barnyard." [O]thers gave it the very proper name of "Uncle Sam[']s Sawmill." The other barn was used or intended for the more slightly wounded. Probing for bullets and dressing of wounds was mainly performed here. As soon as they were tended to they were put out doors on the ground, covered with a blanket and left to themselfes [sic] to indulge in wholesome meditations over the beauties of patriotism and liberty; but such who were able to endure transportation in an ambulance were directly sent back to hospital in Louisville.[73]

A war correspondent saw a similar scene. He reported, "The scenes in the hospitals were equally harrowing. The surgeons were provided with boards on which their patients were lain, and where legs and arms were sawn off with the same *sang froid* which a butcher would manifest in dissecting a beef." L.W. Day of the 101st Ohio Infantry remarked that one operating table, near where there "were several piles of amputated limbs," was simply "an old work-bench." The surgeons were poorly prepared for the aftermath of the battle.[74]

While most structures near the battlefield became hospitals, two of the main field hospitals near the northern end of the field were Antioch Church in Mercer County, which housed Union patients, and the Goodnight farm, where many Confederates from Major General Benjamin F. Cheatham's division recuperated. Dr. Polk, who preached at Antioch Church prior to the war, wrote, "For more than ten days after the battle the field hospitals, except Antioch Church and Mr. Goodnight's farm, were being cleared of the wounded; the two above excepted contained about three hundred of the wounded." As these were two primary hospitals, they deserve some examination.[75]

Antioch Church was a major Union hospital after the Battle of Perryville. The church and surrounding yard were full of wounded troops, and some Federal soldiers who died there were buried in the churchyard. *Courtesy of the Perryville Battlefield State Historic Site.*

When the fighting ended, many of the injured from Union Brigadier General James S. Jackson's 10th Division were taken to Antioch Church. Among them was Adam Johnston of the 79th Pennsylvania, who had been shot below his left knee. At 2:30 p.m. on October 9, twenty-four hours after the fight began, Johnston was hauled to the church, where he and three others were "thrown out in a pile like wood...the church was perfectly filled and [wounded were] under ever shade tree nigh at hand...I lay for six days out under a white oak tree, with my wound dressed once." Johnston's journey is illustrative of circumstances endured by many of the wounded. On October 15, he was moved from the church to a hospital within the city limits of Perryville. Eight days later, he traveled fifteen miles southward to Lebanon, where he stayed for four more days. Transported to Louisville, Johnston entered a hospital at New Albany, Indiana, on November 6. Finally, on January 9, 1863, the soldier left to rejoin his regiment.[76]

The tale of Ormond Hupp of the 5th Indiana Light Artillery also illustrates what many wounded soldiers experienced on the battlefield. Hupp's battery, consisting of ninety soldiers and six cannon, had been posted on a ridge overlooking Doctor's Creek, on the center-right side of the Union line. After enduring an artillery duel and several waves of attacking Confederate infantry, the battery withdrew to the rear. This is when Hupp's troubles started. A horse attached to Hupp's limber was shot and killed. As Hupp tried to unbuckle the dead horse, he wrote, a Rebel artillery shell "struck me on the left arm and passing on, struck the ammunition chest, exploded and caused the cartridges in the chest to explode." One soldier was hit in the head by shrapnel and instantly killed. Four others, including Hupp, suffered horrendous burns, broken limbs and other injuries. Hupp's arms and face were cut. He wrote, "When the chest blew up it took me in the air about ten feet...[I] concluded I was torn to pieces, but after striking the ground and lying there about three minutes, I jumped up and saw that I was badly wounded, my clothes were all torn off, and the burn from the powder set me near crazy."[77]

Blinded by the smoke from the explosion, Hupp, who knew where the brigade hospital was located, decided to walk there before he grew too weak from a loss of blood. After walking a quarter of a mile, a "young man" gave him a drink from a canteen, which "revived" him, and Hupp continued on. He reached the hospital, "a small log house" located behind and to the left of the Union line, which was likely the Widow Gibson cabin or barn. The battle raged around the structure, and Hupp wrote, "Shell and shot were passing all around the house and it [was] afterward struck by a shell, killing two men." Hupp went into the house "to have my wounds dressed, but the surgeon was so frightened that he knew nothing, as he wanted to take my arm off when there was no bone injured." Hupp immediately departed and found another hospital "in a farm house" (possibly the Russell house), but there were three hundred other wounded crowding it. Exhausted from a loss of blood, he collapsed on the road. The artilleryman decided that he would die. He wrote that he "cared for nothing—I was almost crazy through pain."[78]

Miraculously, a soldier in Hupp's battery who had been sent to the rear to find water found Hupp, bathed his head and face, put the wounded man on a horse and took him to another field hospital located a half mile to the rear. While moving in that direction, they encountered "a man that has a tub full of whiskey poured out of a barrel and was giving it to the wounded." Hupp was given "a quart basin full" but was not allowed to drink all of it. "I drank near the quart and felt no effects from it any more than it gave me a new spirit," he wrote.[79]

Finally, Hupp reached another farmhouse that was a hospital. A surgeon dressed his arm and put "sweet oil" on the burns on his face to ease the pain. The doctors then procured "a quilt from the lady of the house" and placed Hupp under a tree. He remained there until the next day. Early on the morning of October 9, Hupp wrote, "Orders came that all those that could must get back about two miles toward [Mackville] to a large meeting house [Antioch Church] that had been converted into a hospital." Riding in his company ambulance, he went to Antioch Church and "lay under a large oak tree till 3 o'clock p.m. without any thing to eat since I was wounded." Hupp's friend eventually visited and made him coffee. Hupp noted, "I laid under this tree two nights with but the one quilt, the weather was quite cold and chilling and in consequence many suffered."[80]

On October 11, one of Hupp's comrades who had been slightly wounded in the caisson explosion arrived to take Hupp to a barn where the battery's wounded had been gathered. He found a horse and took Hupp to the barn. There, he was placed in a straw-covered "shed" and was fed "sheep broth and a cracker." That afternoon, his wounds were dressed. By this point, three days after the battle, his wound "had become very painful, especially my left arm." He remained in the shed for two more days, when he took an ambulance to Perryville, where a "train of wagons" was leaving for Louisville. Placed in one of the ninety wagons, he rode in the open vehicle until they stopped in Springfield at 10:00 p.m. Having traveled fifteen miles,

Hupp wrote, "my sufferings were more than I can express, but I had made up my mind to reach [Louisville] if I lived. There was nothing issued to us and all I had that day was one cracker and I had not slept a wink since the battle so of course I was well nigh exhausted, so when morning came I was glad to see it for I lay rolling in pain all night."[81]

On October 14, one day after leaving Perryville, Hupp had a cup of coffee and a cracker. At 1:00 p.m., he reached Bardstown, where residents gave him more coffee. A local lady dressed his arm, "which was in a fair state of mortification." Leaving Bardstown three hours later, they traveled eight miles and were fed coffee and meat. Again, Hupp could not sleep at all during the night. On the morning of October 15, Hupp wrote, "My wound became very sore, not being washed or dressed once since that fight; I could hardly stand to ride and felt very much exhausted." He was given wine and whiskey and finally reached Louisville at 7:00 a.m. on October 16, eight days after the battle. The wagons did not stop, however, and instead pressed across the Ohio River to New Albany, Indiana. Arriving at 8:30 a.m., they found the New Albany hospitals ready to receive them. Placed in Ward 3 of Hospital #1, which was on Main Street in the Upper City School building, he finally had a bed to sleep in. This was fortunate, for the burned Hupp had only slept about four hours since the battle. There, he ate "a good supper" and "felt myself a new man." He wrote that before midnight his arm was dressed and his wounds "were found to be in a mortifying condition; another day's delay and the amputation of my arm would have been necessary to have saved my life." He was also given morphine and finally slept. By this point, Hupp's family had been told that he was dead, but a friend wrote home to correct the news. Later, his battery commander, Captain Peter Simonson, visited Hupp and brought the wounded soldier a month's worth of supplies.[82]

Hupp wrote, "For the first month after I came to the hospital my sufferings were great, very seldom would I sleep over one hour during the night and often not shut my eyes." By March 1863, five months after the battle, he was still in New Albany, suffering with pain. He was, however, working as a nurse, aiding soldiers who had been wounded at the Battle of Stones River. Hupp's long road to recovery was typical of many of the Perryville wounded.[83]

For injured Union soldiers fighting on their left flank, Antioch Church became a major destination. And, as Hupp notes, several of those fighting on other parts of the field were also taken there. Injured troops were shuttled to the site or simply walked to the house of worship, seeking medical attention. Furthermore, on the morning after the battle, Union authorities sent many

"Every House Was a Hospital"

Cemetery gates at Camp Nelson National Cemetery. The Union army first buried its dead in regimental plots, but these troops were moved to the Perryville National Cemetery, located west of town. After the war, these Federal casualties were again moved to Camp Nelson National Cemetery, located south of Lexington in Jessamine County. Today, many of the Perryville casualties buried there are unknown. *Courtesy of the Kentucky Historical Society.*

wounded troops in that direction, hoping to alleviate crowding from the Perryville hospitals. Several Union men died at the house of worship, and at least thirteen were buried in the churchyard. These included members of the 24th Illinois Infantry, 80th Illinois Infantry, 123rd Illinois Infantry, 1st Michigan Engineers and Mechanics, 2nd Ohio Infantry, 3rd Ohio Infantry, 105th Ohio Infantry and 21st Wisconsin Infantry. Among the men who died from their wounds were Private Albert Richardson of the 80th Illinois and Private George Newsome of the 123rd Illinois, who died on October 29, three weeks after the battle. From that same regiment, Private John Lawrence passed away on October 22, while Private James Pruett died five days after the battle. Private Jerome Smith of the 105th Ohio died at the church on the day of the fight, while nineteen-year-old Buckeye Private John Tucker expired on October 13. Men from other units, including Corporal Aaron Sherwood of the 21st Wisconsin, also lost their lives at the house of worship. The remains of these troops were eventually moved twice; first to the Perryville National Cemetery established west of town (which no longer exists) and finally to the Camp Nelson National Cemetery in Jessamine County, Kentucky. The move was precipitated by shaky land titles and the expense of maintaining the cemetery.[84]

Chapter 5

"LAY HIM DOWN AND LET HIM DIE"

The Confederate troops who faced the Union soldiers who died at Antioch Church were members of Major General Benjamin F. Cheatham's division. Many of Cheatham's wounded were left at the Goodnight farm, about one mile east of the battlefield. According to Cheatham, some of his injured were loaded into wagons and traveled with the retreating army. However, Cheatham wrote, "the balance were left in the old house [Goodnight] and in fence-corners. Dr. [J.R.] Buist was left in charge of them, [and] he built shelters over them with brush and corn-stalks to keep the sun off." Like the Northern troops, the wounded Confederates endured miserable conditions.[85]

While Cheatham's men loaded their wounded comrades into wagons and marched from Perryville, Sam Watkins and several other Rebels spent the night transporting injured soldiers to the Goodnight farm. "We helped bring off a man by the name of Hodge," Watkins wrote, "with his under jaw shot off and his tongue lolling out. We brought off Captain Lute B. [Irwin]. Lute was shot though the lungs and was vomiting blood all the while, and begging us to lay him down and let him die. But Lute is living yet. Also, Lieutenant [Woldridge], with both eyes shot out. I found him rambling in a briar patch."[86]

Despite the severity of the wounds, these patients survived. One, Lewis "Lute" Broyles Irwin, was a well-respected physician who enlisted in Company G of the 1st Tennessee Infantry in the spring of 1861. While campaigning in western Virginia, he was elected captain. After being injured at Perryville, Lute was, according to his obituary, left at the Goodnight farm "with hundreds of other wounded to be surrendered to the enemy. Their bed was straw spread upon the ground in a lot inclosed [*sic*] with a rail fence, their covering the canopy of heaven, which constituted the field hospital." Irwin recovered and returned to the regiment but was unfit to serve in the field. He spent the rest of the war "assigned to post duty." Perryville ended his fighting career.[87]

When Watkins penned his memoirs forty years after the war, Lute was "living yet." Irwin returned to his medical practice and died on September 29, 1909, at the age of seventy-five years and seven months. He was assuredly thankful that Watkins did not "lay him down and let him die" at Perryville.[88]

Watkins also aided Lieutenant John H. Woldridge. Born in Pulaski, Tennessee, on September 20, 1836, Woldridge was educated at Lynneville, Tennessee, and Giles College in Pulaski. Woldridge graduated from law school in Lebanon, Tennessee, in 1858 and joined a private law practice. Upon the outbreak of the Civil War, he and his law partner enlisted in the 1st Tennessee Infantry. Woldridge fought with the unit throughout western Virginia and, at Perryville, led Company K. During the regiment's charge against John Starkweather's troops, the officer was shot through the temple. The bullet severed his optic nerve, blinding him in both eyes.[89]

Ethel Moore was a young woman who traveled with Cheatham's division during much of the war, including the Perryville Campaign. In 1898, while addressing a group of Southern veterans, she recalled Woldridge's sad predicament. "Well do I remember," she said, "after spending all night on the battlefield gathering up the wounded of Cheatham's Division and sending them to the rear, coming at daylight and going back to the Goodnight hospital, some three miles in the rear, finding Lieut. Woldridge lying on the floor with a cloth over the upper part of his face, the sight from both eyes gone forever to this world." Moore, and many of Woldridge's fellow soldiers, believed the wound to be mortal. The blind soldier survived, however, and after the war a United Confederate Veterans' Bivouac in Giles County, Tennessee, was named in his honor. This was quite a distinction, for most bivouacs were named after dead Southern officers. Blind for nearly fifty-one years, Woldridge died on July 22, 1913. According to his obituary, "He exhibited wonderful courage and endurance in his long battle over half a century against the encroachments of this terrible wound. It finally invaded his brain and caused his death." Thus, the Battle of Perryville claimed another victim in the twentieth century.[90]

"Lay Him Down and Let Him Die"

In addition to Ethel Moore, other women traveled with the Confederates during the Kentucky campaign. Perhaps the hardiest of the lot was Mrs. Betsy Sullivan, who was known to Maney's brigade as "Mother Sullivan." Her husband, John, was an Irish immigrant who served in Company K of the 1st Tennessee. Betsy's endurance was stellar, having marched with the regiment since the beginning of the war. According to Tennessean W.W. Cunningham, Mrs. Sullivan, who was in her early thirties at the time of the battle, "was tall and weighed about one hundred and eighty pounds." While the regiment waited at Corinth, Mississippi, before moving toward the Bluegrass State, Company K, which Mrs. Sullivan referred to as "her company," gave her a horse, which she rode into Kentucky. She was a maternal figure for many in the regiment, and the troops cared for her as she cared for them.[91]

When John Sullivan charged Starkweather's position, he received "a hole in his forehead that exposed a part of the brain" and was left for dead on the field. At midnight, Betsy Sullivan, waiting at the Goodnight farm, learned that her husband had been shot. Alone, she took to the field to find him.

Mrs. Sullivan returned to the Goodnight farm several hours later. According to Private Marcus Toney of the 1st Tennessee, Betsy "was a stalwart woman, and brought John on her shoulder to the hospital." Under the meticulous care of his wife, John recovered. Two weeks later, the Sullivans and the blind Woldridge procured a "carryall" to travel to Pulaski, Tennessee. Near Lebanon, Kentucky, however, Union authorities captured the party and sent them to prison. While some sources state that Mrs. Sullivan was incarcerated with her husband, she likely went home to Pulaski to await his return. When John was exchanged and rejoined the regiment, Betsy visited him. Although her disabled husband could not return to the field, Mrs. Sullivan wanted to remain with the regiment. The 1st Tennessee refused, but to thank her for her arduous service, they raised a large sum as a gift. According to Cunningham, the troops gave her $25,000.[92]

Although Bragg's army left Perryville, several Confederates remained behind to find and care for the wounded. Among them was Marcus Toney. "It was a sad sight that night as I gazed upon the upturned, ghastly faces of our dead," Toney wrote, "and the cries of the wounded for 'water!' 'water!' 'water!' was heartrending." Just as soldiers commonly recalled the Confederate dead piled up in pens, they also remembered the wounded troops calling for water. A veteran of the 50th Ohio Infantry wrote, "I remember that all through the night I could hear the poor, wounded boys calling for water." Confederate W.H. Davis wrote, "No man ever experienced such a night of torture as we did listening to our wounded comrades, prostrate on the hot earth, crying for water." Evan Davis of the 21st Wisconsin recalled, "I well remember the pitiful cry for water from the parched mouths of our wounded and dying comrades when we had none to give."[93]

Upon reaching the battlefield, Toney found dozens of dead from his regiment. His Company B had lost fourteen killed and thirteen wounded while charging Union guns that anchored the Federals' left flank. Among the dead was one of Toney's "intimate friends," Robert S. Hamilton. A native Kentuckian who worked as a proofreader in Nashville, Hamilton joined the 1st Tennessee at age eighteen. Although Hamilton's bluegrass family was divided over the war, Robert was an avid secessionist. During one of the final charges against the Union position, he was shot in the forehead and killed.

Toney knew that Hamilton had relatives in Lexington, forty miles from the battlefield. From the light of a burning barn, Toney wrote Hamilton's sister-in-law, Mrs. Wesley C. Hamilton, a simple note: "Robert was killed in [a] gallant charge this evening. Will take care of [his] remains until you arrive." Toney recalled that he did not write Robert's brother because Wesley "was a Union man, and Robert never wrote a line to him; but all his correspondence was with his sister-in-law." Battlefield animosities faded with the sun. Toney wrote that soldiers "blue and gray mingled together all that night removing the wounded," and one of the Federals agreed to deliver the note to Mrs. Hamilton.[94]

That night, Toney buried twenty-seven members of the 1st Tennessee in a gully near where they had fallen. Using a Federal breastplate, he scooped dirt over the corpses, burying Hamilton at the head of the line. One wonders how Toney performed this sad duty. The memory of interring more than a score of his comrades must have haunted him forever. Of those known to have been buried there, seven were from Company A, fourteen were from Company B and one was from Company C.[95]

Toney returned to the Goodnight farm, where he cared for eight wounded comrades, including the blind Woldridge and Lute Irwin. Their wounds were horrible enough to be remembered by Toney, Sam Watkins and Charles Quintard, the chaplain of the 1st Tennessee. Toney exclaimed that "Woldridge lost both of his eyes" and that Irwin was "badly wounded." Nursing them at the Goodnight farm proved to be strenuous. "For three nights," he wrote, "I did not close my eyes in sleep." Quintard also worked diligently, recalling that from 3:00 p.m.

"Lay Him Down and Let Him Die"

until half past five the next morning, without food of any sort, I was incessantly occupied with the wounded. It was a horrible night I spent,— God save me from such another. I suppose excitement kept me up. About half past five in the morning of the 9ᵗʰ, I dropped—I could do no more. I went out by myself and leaning against a fence, I wept like a child. And all that day I was so unnerved that if any one asked me about the regiment [1ˢᵗ Tennessee], I could make no reply without tears. Having taken off my shirt to tear into strips to make bandages, I took a severe cold.[96]

On October 11, Mrs. Hamilton arrived from Lexington with a hearse and casket for her deceased brother-in-law. She also brought blankets and food for the wounded Confederates. Toney guided her across the Goodnight farm, past the Walker house, through the dried Chaplin River and over the corpse-strewn battlefield, where hogs were rooting up bodies and knocking down the rail barricades protecting the unburied corpses. When they reached the graves of the 1ˢᵗ Tennessee, Toney raked the dirt away from Robert's face. "Mrs. Hamilton," the Confederate said, "this is Robert."

With Robert Hamilton disfigured from both the wound and decomposition, Mrs. Hamilton was shocked at the sight. Drawing her breath, she asked, "Is it possible that these are Robert's remains?"

To persuade her, Toney lifted one of Robert's hands from the ground. Brushing the dirt away, Toney displayed Robert's fingers. Apparently, whenever Robert was deep in thought, he bit his fingernails, sometimes chewing them so short that he drew blood. When Mrs. Hamilton saw the clipped fingernails, she recognized her brother-in-law's remains, thanked Toney and returned to Lexington. Robert was interred in the Lexington Cemetery, where he is the only known Confederate casualty from the Battle of Perryville.[97]

Robert was killed by Federal troops, but his family still supported the Union cause. Robert's brother, John W. Hamilton, joined the 18ᵗʰ Kentucky (Union) Infantry Regiment in March 1864. Therefore, nearly two years after Robert was shot by Federal troops, his brother enlisted in the Union army. John survived the war but died in 1867 at age thirty-seven. Both brothers, who fought on opposing sides, are interred in the Hamilton family plot in Section C, Lot 16, of the Lexington Cemetery. Standing at the plot is a moving experience that details the fratricidal nature of the Civil War in Kentucky. The brothers' adjacent tombstones show their respective sides. The bottom of Robert's grave lists "CSA," while John's headstone is inscribed "USA."

These two brothers, who fought on opposite sides, are now united in burial. They served different causes but share the same ground.[98] Thanks to the work of soldier-nurses like Toney, some of the wounded Confederates at the Goodnight farm survived. One fortunate soldier was Lieutenant James I. Hall of the 9th Tennessee Infantry. After Hall's regiment swept over Union Lieutenant Charles Parsons's artillery battery, the Tennessean was wounded in the torso. He lay on the battlefield all evening and was taken to the Goodnight farm near midnight. He later wrote:

> *The surgeons, on examination, pronounced my wound necessarily mortal and I was placed on the ground under an apple tree between two men whose wounds were similar to mine. A liberal dose of morphine was given to each one of us and I remember its soothing effect on me. The other two men were suffering intensely from their wounds and knowing that my wound was similar to theirs kept me awake for a long time by asking me such questions as "how I felt" and "whether I thought I could last through the night." I finally got to sleep and when I awoke the next morning, I had a corpse at each elbow. The men had died while I slept. Contrary to the predictions of the surgeons, I was still alive.*[99]

Hall remained outside for several days, his condition exacerbated because his clothes had been ripped away by the doctors who examined his wound. Exposed to the elements, he was eventually placed under a hastily constructed lean-to made from old planks. The crude shelter helped, he later wrote, because "a heavy snow fell greatly to the discomfort of our men in the hospital, since they weren't all provided with shelter and clothing. A large number of our men, however, were taken to the homes of the good people in the country in Harrodsburg and Danville." Immediately after the battle, citizens from the region traveled to the hospitals and distributed food, clothing and blankets. For example, Southern sympathizer Florence Goalder and her sister, both from Green County, Kentucky, scoured their area for supplies and rode forty miles to deliver them to wounded Confederates.[100]

Hall remained at the Goodnight farm for approximately two weeks. Surprisingly, this Rebel's savior was a Unionist. Colonel Joshua Barbee of Danville, a member of one of the town's most prominent families, sent his carriage to Perryville and retrieved Hall. It was déjà vu for the Tennessean because the injured officer had boarded at Barbee's home, a Greek Revival mansion on the east end of Danville, when he was a

Danville, located about ten miles from the battlefield, had several private schools during the Civil War era, including the Danville Female Academy. This building may have been a hospital, and the school's students undoubtedly took food, medicine and supplies to sick soldiers in town after the Battle of Perryville. *Courtesy of Centre College.*

student at Centre College. Taken to Barbee's residence, Hall was, he wrote, "placed in the room which I had occupied fifteen years earlier while a student at Centre College and was treated with unremitting kindness by Colonel B. and his family."[101]

This convalescence became a homecoming when several of Hall's school-day acquaintances, most of them Unionists, visited him. These included Centre College professors and the president of the college, who later died from an illness contracted while helping sick Federal soldiers. Hall, who was indebted to Barbee for the rest of his life, wrote, "I want to mention the fact that Mr. Barbee, although a pronounced Union man, in befriending and sheltering me, was in danger of bringing suspicion on his loyalty."[102]

Hall remained there for more than two months. Finally, after pulling strings with former Centre College classmates, Hall secured a parole for himself and several wounded comrades. His return surprised his loved ones. Hall's wound had been pronounced mortal, and newspapers and official reports noted that the officer had died. The lieutenant's family read about his supposed demise in the newspapers. Later, Hall recalled that his family and friends

> *had no hope of ever seeing me again. The only one who seemed inclined to discredit the report was my six year old daughter who could not be convinced that I was dead and would say to her grandmother: "Grandma, Papa's not dead. He'll come home one of these days, now you'll see." When I finally reached home, arriving there in the dusk of evening, I found her standing alone on the porch—seemingly waiting for me. Her greeting was: "why here's Papa," and then to her Aunt Sarah, "I told you he would come back."[103]*

Most children of the missing were not so fortunate. There were hundreds of families who never knew what became of their fathers, sons and brothers. Several rows of unknown men buried in Harrodsburg, Camp Nelson, Danville, Lebanon and other communities attest to this fact. Most of the dead interred under the Confederate monument that stands over the mass grave at the Perryville Battlefield State Historic Site are unknown. As late as 1900, a note in the December issue of *Confederate Veteran* stated, "Mrs. W.M. Ritchey, of Athlone, Cal., seeks information on her brother, Isaac Cunningham, who was lost in the battle of Perryville." It is likely that Mrs. Cunningham never learned of Isaac's fate, although her sadness and curiosity had lingered for nearly forty years.[104]

If relatives were fortunate to secure news about their family members in the army, it usually took weeks. Surprisingly, the wife of Captain Mark L. Evans of the 8th Texas Cavalry heard several reports of her husband's death. On October 21, 1862, gunsmith Benjamin Mills of Harrodsburg—who had been master armorer at Harpers Ferry and abducted by John Brown during Brown's 1859 raid—wrote Maria Evans:

> *It has fallen to my lot to inform you of the melancholy fate of your lamented husband, and may God help you and give you fortitude in your bereavement.*

"Lay Him Down and Let Him Die"

Capt. Evans was ordered into the battle of Perryville on the 8ᵗʰ inst. to charge a battery, which he did most gallantly. But he received a fatal wound in the head by a Minie ball which fractured his skull. He was brought to my home, where he had good attention until the 18ᵗʰ inst., when at forty minutes past six he expired. He lay in a drowsy state all the time, and never opened his eyes; he talked very little, and his talk was like a man who is very drowsy. His Masonic brothers helped to get his coffin and to bury him. He and Col. McDaniel, of [the 41ˢᵗ Georgia], were buried at the same time. Their bodies now lie in the Masonic grounds where they can be removed.

Mills also informed Mrs. Evans that "the Indian boy [Evans's body servant] attended him most faithfully. My wife has his clothes, a ring, and a lock of his hair, which will all be kept for you."[105]

A few weeks later, Lieutenant Frank Batchelor of the 8ᵗʰ Texas wrote another painful notice to Mrs. Evans. Batchelor related that after Mark had been shot in the head, Mark's brother and two others transported him to Harrodsburg. The letter stated that Evans "was struck by a large-sized musket ball just above the right temple and ranged over the skull, tearing the flesh out some four inches and a half in length by one [inch] in width and leaving the skull bare and slightly fractured." With little hope that Mark would survive, Batchelor delayed the descriptive "letter till the announcement of your husband's death appeared in the Louisville papers."[106]

Despite these somber reports, there were some stories of survival. Private Edward Elam of the 9ᵗʰ Tennessee had his leg amputated after the battle and lived until 1881. Another member of the regiment, Private Alford Ward, lost his right leg, and he, too, survived. A third soldier in the 9ᵗʰ, Private George McDill, was shot through the lungs and lived until 1898. Just as miraculous is the story of Captain John M. Taylor of the 27ᵗʰ Tennessee. Taylor received four wounds at Perryville. Shot through both thighs, his right femur was shattered and he was disabled for life. Taylor became a judge and lived for many more years. One of the most intriguing tales of survival, however, involved twenty-one-year-old Robert T. Bond of the 9ᵗʰ Tennessee. Bond had been wounded at the Battle of Shiloh. At Perryville, he was wounded six times and survived. He eventually rejoined the command and was again injured while fighting near Atlanta. Despite eight wounds received in Confederate service, Bond survived the war.[107]

Eventually, the Union army arrived at the Goodnight farm and cared for the wounded Confederates left there. John A. Martin of the 8ᵗʰ Kansas

Infantry described the scene. "As we pressed on evidences of a hasty flight were manifest," Martin penned. "Their dead and wounded were left uncared for, and the ground was covered with guns, blankets and knapsacks, indicating the confusion in which they had fled." Unionist Wilbur Hinman likely visited this area when he wrote:

Lying upon the ground, with no shelter from the fierce heat of the sun by day or the dew by night, were some three hundred rebel wounded. They had as yet received no care from the surgeons. Many of them were in the most horrible condition that the mind can conceive. Some were shot through the head, body or limbs, others mangled by fragments of shell, and all suffering the greatest torments. We gave them water, and shared with them the contents of our haversacks, but there was nothing else that we could do. Words are powerless to convey an adequate idea of these harrowing scenes.

Several weeks after the battle, the field hospital was closed, and the remaining wounded were sent to Harrodsburg or Danville. Of the unknown number of Confederates who died from their wounds at the Goodnight farm, most were buried in the Goodnight family cemetery, a tree-encased plot located several hundred yards from the farmhouse. As these Southerners were prisoners of war when they died, the United States erected a monument to the unknown dead buried there.[108]

Despite the horrors of the aftermath, a handful of men found happiness amidst the anguish. Two soldiers from the 9th Tennessee, Willie Holmes and James Peter, were wounded during the battle. After spending time recovering at the Goodnight farm, they were sent to the house of a Mr. Messick in Danville. Here, Holmes met a Miss More, whom he eventually married. Another member of the brigade, Daniel Risdon Smith of Company C, 27th Tennessee, also found local love. Like Toney, Smith remained behind to care for his wounded comrades at the Goodnight farm. According to his pension file, Smith "was absolutely the last Confederate soldier who was at the Goodknight [sic] hospital." While in Perryville, Smith met and married Minerva Bugg. He never returned to the Confederate army. The couple lived in nearby Dixville for the rest of their lives, and some of their descendants reside in the area to this day.[109]

Chapter 6
"BROKEN IN SPIRIT"

At Antioch Church, the Goodnight farm and other hastily organized hospitals across the area, surgical operations began as soon as the injured were removed from the field. E.L. Davison was a Springfield resident who followed the Union army ten miles from his hometown to Perryville. After watching the battle, Davison stumbled upon a makeshift field hospital where, despite his lack of medical training, he volunteered as a surgical assistant. As the doctors furiously amputated limbs, Davison administered what little chloroform was available and cut off clothing to expose the wounds. Davison was prepping a soldier with a knee wound when Davison's minister, the Reverend Miles Sanders, arrived to help. Davison wrote, "The bone was sawed off and naturally flew up (it not being held tight enough) spinning blood over everything; Sanders fell over in a faint." For civilians who had never witnessed the horrors of warfare, the aftermath of battle was a rude awakening.[110]

Shortly after the Union flanks collapsed toward the Dixville Crossroads, Union brigade commander Colonel George Penny Webster was grievously wounded. Several of Webster's soldiers, including Duncan Milner of the 98th Ohio, carried their injured commander to a house that had been converted into a field hospital. Milner wrote:

We carried him thru the crowds of wounded, who covered the ground all around the house, and got him into a corner of a room, the floor of which was lined with the wounded. Here the ball was taken out. It had entered the right side of the right hip, passed through the lower part of his body, and had lodged on the inside of the skin on the left side of the left hip. It was easily cut out...It was a dreadful place to be in; the shrieks and groans of the wounded were awful.

Webster eventually died from his painful wound.[111]

On the morning after the battle, the 41st Ohio Infantry Regiment moved into the Confederates' abandoned lines. Their regimental historian later recorded, "One of the scenes on this advance was a Confederate field hospital in and about a small farm house. The long porch was crowded with wounded men, and just as the regiment passed the surgeons were taking off, near the shoulder, the arm of a poor fellow. Two attendants held the writhing man while the surgeons carved him—for they had no anesthetics to put him into kind insensibility."[112]

Union surgeons who arrived after the fight were overwhelmed by the condition of the hospitals. Dr. J.G. Hatchitt first visited the Russell House, near the crossroads. "I found about one hundred and fifty wounded," the doctor wrote, "most of them lying on the ground in the yard, and no surgeon, except Surgeon G.D. Beebe, U.S.V., medical director of McCook's corps, and three or four from the 1st division. They had labored all night as best they could. No supplies having reached this hospital, they were compelled to amputate without chloroform." Hatchitt also discovered that the drought caused severe sanitation problems. Hospitals north of town needed water more than the hospitals west or south of town. "Some surgeons told me that they could not get water enough to wash the blood from their hands for two days," he wrote. With no water to clean hands or instruments, post-injury complications and deaths were common.[113]

Amputations, with or without anesthesia, were dangerous, and many did not survive these operations. Bliss Morse of the 105th Ohio informed his mother that "Lucius Prouty died Sunday after having his leg amputated near the hip. He laid on the field one night, and day, after the fight. The Rebels gave him water while he laid on the field." There were scores of similar stories, and several men from the 15th Kentucky died of tetanus.[114]

As Hatchitt explained, water remained scarce, and troops went to great lengths to find it. Immediately after the fight, one drought-stricken Georgian was so thirsty that he and his comrades "drank copiously of soap suds from the wash tubs." Confederate John W. Henderson of Buckner's division, who was "afraid to ask to hunt water," heard General Buckner say that he was thirsty. As an excuse to get his own water, Henderson took Buckner's canteen and filled it from a stagnant pond. In 1889, he wrote Buckner, telling his former commander that he was afraid "you would ask me where I got [the water,] for there were a great many dead and wounded lying around the pool...whose wounds had been washed in the same." Soldiers and officers alike endured trying circumstances after the fight, and many of these men died from illnesses contracted during the campaign, brought about by these conditions.[115]

A lack of supplies worsened the already dreadful hospital conditions. When the Union army stormed down from Louisville, General Buell ordered that only one ambulance should accompany each brigade (at Perryville, the average Union brigade numbered 2,161 men). Therefore, when the wounded were collected, Federal surgeons were woefully unprepared for the thousands of casualties. Captain John Inskeep of the 17th Ohio recorded that "the medical Dept. was sadly deficient in the means to properly care for the wounded," while an Indiana soldier remarked that "the regimental surgeons found themselves with more patients than they could properly attend to, and the poor fellows suffered much, both from the inability of the surgeons to get round and for the want of medical supplies." In fact, some doctors believed that Buell's order caused unnecessary suffering and even a loss of life. These problems were reported by the *New Albany Daily Ledger*, which, on October 20, claimed, "The condition of the sick and wounded at Chaplin Hills [Perryville] is said to be absolutely wretched. They are without the most ordinary necessaries. The surgeons left there are either incompetent, criminally negligent, or brutally cruel." Although conditions were unacceptable, the newspaper's assessment of the surgeons is unfair. The overwhelmed doctors did what they could with little or no supplies, and many residents worked without rest to care for the injured. One officer told the paper, however, that "the condition of the sick and wounded remaining there is enough to excite the indignation of the whole country against those whose duty it is to provide for these brave men." For Buell's order decreasing the number of ambulances, the fault lies with him.[116]

Many surgeons commented on the lack of medicines. Union Dr. G.G. Shumard reported that because of Buell's order, "the supply thus conveyed was altogether insufficient to meet the wants of the sick." J.S. Newberry, the secretary for the Western Department of the U.S. Sanitary Commission, informed his superiors that

> *the condition of the wounded in this fight was particularly distressing. No adequate provision had been made for their care. The stock of medicines*

and hospital stores in the hands of the surgeons was insignificant. They had almost no ambulances, no tents, no hospital furniture, and no proper food. In addition to this, the small village of Perryville afforded but very imperfect means for the care of the great number of wounded concentrated there, either in the way of buildings to be used as hospitals, or resources and appliances of any other kind.

Dr. Read of the Sanitary Commission concurred. "There had been almost no preparation for the care of the wounded at Perryville, and as a consequence the suffering from want of *help* of all kinds, as well as proper accommodations, food, medicines, and hospital stores, was excessive. For this state of things, however, the surgeons are not to blame...the fault lies higher than they." Read, and others, placed the blame squarely on Buell's shoulders.[117]

For weeks after the battle, the lack of wood and water enhanced the surgeons' difficulties. Dr. Hatchitt remarked, "It was necessary to go occasionally from six to ten miles for forage, so much had the country been stripped by the armies, and sometimes it was necessary to seize both wood and forage at the point of the bayonet." The Union army attempted to alleviate this suffering by sending bandages, medicines and other supplies from Louisville, but a bureaucratic quartermaster at Bardstown, thirty miles west of Perryville, held the items for two weeks before forwarding them. Luckily for the sick and wounded, the Sanitary Commission sent twenty-one wagons to Perryville, each containing kegs of butter, live chickens, bandages and other medical supplies. Several surgeons from the Cincinnati branch of the Sanitary Commission also traveled with these supplies, but for an unknown reason, they "refused to co-operate with Dr. Read, in the distribution of the stores."[118]

The drought hindered the surgeons' efforts, led to thousands of thirsty troops and affected the hospitals' sanitation. It is certain that these unsanitary surroundings led to scores of deaths from disease and other complications. The drought lasted past the battle, and much of the water in town had to be hauled from two springs located more than a mile from Perryville. This lack of water caused illnesses. Union Private Jonathan McElderry, who remained at Perryville in camp for several weeks, wrote that "we have the camp diarea [*sic*] very bad among uss [*sic*] now it is a troublesome disease harde [*sic*] to check and very painfull [*sic*]." Shortages and illnesses continued in Perryville until the last hospitals closed there on March 23, 1863, more than five months after the battle.[119]

Shortages also affected the town's civilian population. When the fighting began, residents were displaced from their homes and local farms were occupied. Citizens grew fearful as their winter stores were depleted by the sick and wounded. At one residence, Read recalled, "the occupants were very poor, but doing all in their power for those in their charge. The mother of the family promised to continue to do so, but said, with tears in her eyes, she feared that she and her children must starve when the winter came."[120]

The home of one local woman was literally caught in the crossfire during the battle, inducing her to leave the area after the fight. On October 9, Cincinnati war correspondent Alf Burnett walked the field. As he traveled the ravaged pastures, Burnett reached a small, two-room log house. "The chimney had been partly torn away by a cannonball," Burnett wrote. "A shell had struck the roof of the building, ripping open quite a gutter in the rafters. A dead horse lay in the little yard directly in front of the house, actually blocking the doorway, while shot and shell were scattered in every direction about the field in front and rear of this solitary homestead."

Burnett saw "a long, lank, lean woman" hurrying away from the cabin with two young children in tow. She balanced an upside-down table, full of

This barn owned by widow Mary Jane Gibson was located near the center of the Union line. This structure was likely one of the many makeshift hospitals found on the battlefield. *Courtesy of the Perryville Battlefield State Historic Site.*

bedding and household goods, on her head. This widow, whose husband had died of measles prior to the fight, was fleeing from the horrors of the aftermath of battle. When the fighting had raged around her home, she took an axe, chopped a hole in the floor and hid between the joists until the firing stopped. Terrified, she and her children remained there for hours. The battle over and her farmland covered with the dead and wounded, the widow was leaving as fast as she could.[121]

Another woman in Perryville departed during the fight but returned to find her home ransacked. Harriet Karrick, a widow who lived in a stately brick home in downtown Perryville with her eight children and several slaves, left her residence the day before the battle. Upon her return a few days later, Karrick discovered that all of her fencing had been burned for firewood, her outbuildings were full of wounded and sick soldiers, the spring behind her house was nearly drained dry and her home was full of Federal doctors, who used it as their quarters for more than six months. Furthermore, her residence was left in shambles as soldiers searched for coffee, sugar and valuables, and all of the family's clothing was shredded for use as bandages.[122]

The life of another local resident, Perryville Dr. Jefferson J. Polk, was also overturned. Polk was a local physician who, by 1862, had retired because of pulmonary difficulties. When thousands of sick and wounded were deposited in Perryville, however, Polk was forced out of retirement. A staunch Unionist, eight to ten wounded convalesced in his home, and the doctor was appointed surgeon to a Federal field hospital. This hospital, a barn, housed forty Union patients. The sixty-year-old doctor worked until his health nearly failed him.[123]

Although Polk strongly espoused the Federal cause, he was willing to set aside his political convictions in the face of human suffering. The doctor came to the aid of Dr. Karl Langenbecker, a Prussian-born physician who had immigrated to the South prior to the Civil War. After the Battle of Perryville, Langenbecker, a Confederate surgeon with the 13th Louisiana Infantry Regiment, remained behind to care for wounded Rebels in the Perryville Christian Church, which was one of the main Southern hospitals in town. Langenbecker fell ill, and Polk placed the surgeon in his home, where Langenbecker died on December 21. Local legend holds that Polk had the Confederate doctor buried in his own family plot in Perryville's Hillcrest Cemetery. For this doctor, professional courtesy overrode political beliefs.[124]

The family of Charles King Kirkland, whose home was located near some of the heaviest fighting, also experienced these horrors. When the battle started, the Kirklands left their home and visited relatives in Casey County, south of Perryville. Upon their return, they discovered that their house was occupied as a hospital and that most of their furniture had been smashed and burned. Only four pieces remained, including a blood-covered cherry table used as an operating platform. Their clothes were ripped for bandages, their outbuildings were dismantled and burned and their chickens, cows and hogs were consumed. According to one family history, "Soldiers were buried all over the yard. After a rain, hands and feet could be seen as the men were buried so poorly." Mrs. Kirkland refused to live on this farm, and the family eventually moved to Casey County, where Kirkland descendants still live to this day. The battle permanently displaced this family.[125]

While hundreds of residents suffered from the battle, perhaps no one lost more than Henry P. Bottom, a local cabinetmaker and justice of the peace. The forty-seven-year-old Bottom, who owned most of the land upon which the battle was fought, could never have foreseen the carnage that struck his farm. Bottom's house was literally caught in the crossfire on the Union right flank, and bullet holes pocked the home's wooden siding. Furthermore, his home served as a field hospital where, according to one eyewitness, a pile of amputated arms and legs, "some with shoes on, others with socks," stood "four or five feet high." Bottom never recovered, either economically or psychologically, from the horrors and destruction of the Battle of Perryville. Many of his losses were caused when his barn was ignited by an artillery shell. Wounded Union troops had perished in the flames, and after the battle, the barn fire spread to a rail fence. Several dead Federals were under the burning rails, the flames charring their corpses. A captain in Confederate General Simon Bolivar Buckner's division retrieved the bodies and extinguished the flames.[126]

When the Union army regained control of the battlefield, Bottom's home was converted into a field hospital. Dr. McMeens of the 3rd Ohio was the acting brigade surgeon for Lytle's brigade. He first established a hospital in "a small farm house," likely the Bottom house, and adjoining outbuildings that were closest to his regiment's casualties. But, a veteran recalled, "in less time than it takes to pen these lines, after the first arrival of wounded, all the space in and out of doors on the premises was occupied." When one soldier from the 3rd Ohio returned to the Bottom house, he wrote, "Here we found about one hundred men of the 3rd [Ohio] and 15th Kentucky lying stiff and

Confederate troops stormed past the home of Henry P. Bottom as they attacked the right flank of Union Major General Alexander McCook's corps. During the fight, Bottom's barn, located immediately north of the structure, was hit by an artillery shell and burst into flames. Several Union wounded who had crawled into the barn for protection perished in the subsequent fire. After the battle, dead soldiers were buried in Bottom's yard, the home was a hospital and a witness said that a pile of amputated arms and legs stood four or five feet high. *Courtesy of the Perryville Battlefield State Historic Site.*

cold besides many wounded which are carried off tenderly. Trenches were dug, the dead buried."[127]

On the same day, the 81st Indiana camped near Bottom's residence. George Morris of that regiment wove a striking picture of the aftermath of the fight near Bottom's home and Doctor's Creek:

> *Between our regiment and the creek the enemy's wounded lay in every fence corner. Our boys behaved themselves, and treated them kindly, bringing water whenever they desired it. They were mostly Tennessee troops. Some of them deserved no compassion, for they spoke impudently and disdainfully. Nevertheless, on account of their wounds, no notice was taken of it. Down at the creek was a farm house that had been turned into a hospital. The doctors were hard at work at a table, amputating limbs. The yard was full of*

wounded men, lying in rows, covered up with blankets, shrieking with pain, and some lying there were dead. Close to the house was the body of a rebel major, in a corner of the fence. His face was covered. He was neatly dressed in gray cloth. At a short distance to the left was another house used for the same purpose [likely the Chatham House or the Widow Bottom Cabin], *the yard of which was filled with dead, laid in rows. Close to the fence were piles of arms and legs. It was a ghastly sight to look upon. Most of the dead were black in the face, which caused them to look more frightful. A battery of cannon lay dismantled near this house* [probably Palmer's Georgia Battery, which was shot to pieces near the Widow Bottom Cabin]. *In fact, all around the place for hundreds of yards, everything showed plainly that a hard battle had been fought.*[128]

Because of immediate property damages and financial losses, several residents approached Federal authorities in an attempt to secure reparations for stolen or confiscated livestock and goods. William Wade recalled one civilian who went "over to the paymaster about setting pay for [destroyed] fencing and all he got was a cursing." Of these residents, none suffered more than Henry P. Bottom.[129]

Shortly after the battle, Bottom filed a claim for damages against the United States. Since the Federal government would not pay for property damaged during the fighting or for property that was confiscated by the Confederates, Bottom hoped to be reimbursed for goods taken and damaged by Union soldiers. The Federal government, however, would reimburse only citizens whose loyalty to the Union was unquestioned. This point proved to be a hindrance to his efforts.

Bottom's claim shows the devastating impact that the Battle of Perryville had on both the farm and Bottom, who also suffered through the ordeal of burying hundreds of Confederate dead. The battle, for example, completely decimated the family's resources. For the first time ever, the Bottom family had to buy food to eat. According to the claim, Bottom lost nine cows, thirty sheep, 8,540 pounds of pork, 4,500 pounds of bacon, 320 cords of wood (constituting more than 1,300 panels of worm fencing, with each panel being nine rails high with ten-foot-long rails), 3,020 bushels of corn, twenty-two tons of hay, fifty bushels of oats and two horses. The value of the lost items totaled more than $4,800. Henry's son said that the family "didn't get a bushel of corn from the entire one-hundred and twenty-five acres that was planted."[130]

One reason for the profusion of goods on Bottom's farm (despite the horrible autumn drought) is that Bottom had several tenant farmers living on his property at the time of the battle. One resident said that "a good many" tenants were making their living off Bottom's land. Perryvillian Joseph Hafley said that "at the time of the battle Bottom had 75 acres of his own in corn and had 20 or 25 acres rented out; of that rented out...Bottom got one-half" of the crop as rent payment. Hafley added, "Mr. Bottom had in a bigger corn crop in the year of 1862 than before, for they cleared up the hillsides for cultivation."[131]

Despite the many witnesses who attested to Bottom's loyalty to the Union, Bottom's claim was denied. Several witnesses argued that Bottom had to be loyal because he was an elected justice of the peace and county magistrate. Since Boyle County was a Unionist county, they posited, Bottom would not have been elected had he been a Southern sympathizer. It appears, however, that several prominent citizens—including staunch Unionist Dr. Jefferson J. Polk and Bottom's cousin T.W. Bottom—testified that Henry was a Southern sympathizer. Although these residents, according to testimony, disliked Bottom (one, Wilson Green, was called a "bitter enemy of Bottom," and Bottom and Polk were not on speaking terms), their words were heavily considered. Because of this testimony against Henry, and because it was impossible to prove that Union soldiers alone took or destroyed Bottom's property (despite much testimony to the contrary),[132] the two-part claim was dismissed in January 1868 and June 1878. The family received a second chance when the claim was presented to the U.S. Congress. Heard by the Congressional Committee on War Claims, it was, however, "dismissed for want of prosecution," likely meaning that it was dismissed because too much time had lapsed and the claimants were not aggressively pursuing the case. Bottom never received a penny for the thousands of dollars lost from the Battle of Perryville. His descendants, however, who reopened the claim in 1902, were aided when Bottom posthumously had his loyalty affirmed on March 7, 1904. The family finally received $1,715 in 1914, more than fifty years after the battle.[133]

Henry died on September 29, 1901, and was buried in a small family cemetery located less than a mile from the mass grave where, thirty-nine years before, he interred a majority of the Confederate dead. Although the Battle of Perryville irrevocably altered his life, Bottom is remembered for surviving the adversity that was thrust on him by Kentucky's largest Civil War battle. Also important, he stoically endured his losses. Perryville resident

"Broken in Spirit"

Of the Perryville residents who suffered from the aftermath of the battle, perhaps none suffered like Henry P. Bottom, pictured here at age ninety. As a result of the fight, Bottom lost nine cows, thirty sheep, thousands of pounds of pork and bacon, 1,300 panels of worm fencing, 3,020 bushels of corn, twenty-two tons of hay, 50 bushels of oats and two horses. Bottom also buried many of the Confederate dead. One resident said that Bottom "was broken in spirit from that time on until he died." *Courtesy of the Perryville Battlefield State Historic Site.*

M. Cummins stated that Bottom never complained but only expressed worry that his farm "was badly torn up and did not know how he could ever go to house-keeping again."[134]

The damages that Bottom sustained—economically and psychologically—were aptly described by Dr. John Bolling, a local physician. When the government heard Bottom's war claim, Bolling was asked, "Did Mr. Henry P. Bottom ever recover from the losses which he suffered at that time?" Bolling replied, "No sir, he never did. He was broken in spirit from that time on until he died."[135]

Chapter 7
"A SIGHT I NEVER WISH TO SEE AGAIN"

J
ust as local homes and farms were commandeered as field hospitals, so, too, were Perryville institutions. Schools, businesses and churches were hastily converted into cramped, poorly ventilated hospitals, with little medical supplies or attention. Damages to the Ewing Institute, an all-girls' school that Kentucky historian J. Winston Coleman called "one of the country's noted ante-bellum girls' schools," is emblematic of what most Perryville institutions experienced after the battle.[136]

Founded in the 1840s and housed in a brick Greek Revival building on the east side of town, the Ewing Institute had seventy-five female students by 1856. Tuition costs ran from fourteen to thirty-two dollars per session, unless a student elected to take lessons in needlework, piano, pastel drawing or ornamental leatherwork. These electives carried an extra cost.[137] By the early 1860s, fifteen trustees oversaw the school's operations, and when Confederate General Braxton Bragg passed through Perryville before the battle, students from the Ewing Institute serenaded him.[138]

When Bragg returned for the fight, the school did not escape the havoc. The building became crammed with Federal casualties, and damages from the occupation were severe. Local housekeeper Harriett Sandifer noted, "The soldiers used it as a hospital and they tore it up very much." The post and rail fence that surrounded the property was burned for firewood. Sandifer said that the troops "never left a rail or plank." Soldiers tore plaster from the walls and partitions, destroyed stoves, smashed windows and shutters, removed doors from their hinges, soiled paint and piled the school

Students from the Ewing Institute, a noted antebellum school, serenaded Confederate General Braxton Bragg sometime prior to the Battle of Perryville. After the fight, the school became a makeshift hospital. It was severely damaged by the occupation, but the institution survived for many more years. *Courtesy of the Perryville Battlefield Preservation Association.*

desks in the yard for firewood or other uses. Sandifer, who dutifully went to the institute every day during the Union occupation, recalled that the building "was tore all to pieces. The desks that were not burned were abused so." Perryville farmer and businessman C.T. Armstrong, whose brother was a school trustee, believed that desks were pushed together to serve as bunks for the wounded. He added, "The property was all more or less abused."[139]

The occupation lasted for several months. Because the number of wounded and sick in town abated as men died or recovered, Federal authorities first abandoned the private residences that served as hospitals. Second, they vacated local churches and, lastly, other businesses and institutions. Several local residents, including Harriett Sandifer, C.T. Armstrong and merchant William Huston Parks, recalled that the Ewing Institute served as a hospital until April 1863, more than six months after the Battle of Perryville.[140]

The Ewing Institute suffered financially during the war, and after the conflict the school sold off part of its lot. These sales were likely made to cover the cost of repairs and to replace monetary losses caused by declining enrollments.[141] In time, however, the school recovered. In the 1880s and 1890s, enrollment spiked when the school opened its doors to male pupils. Approximately 120 students from the region attended the school, which boasted five teachers. In 1892, it cost the Broyles family $3.50 a month to send their daughter Gay to the Institute. Gay Broyles took reading, writing, spelling, geography, arithmetic, grammar and history. During this time, the institute even offered a family rate for tuition. Any family that sent three children to the school could send their fourth child free of charge.[142]

In early 1907, the trustees of the Ewing Institute sought reparations for losses incurred during the post-battle occupation. When the trustees petitioned the Federal government, they noted that Union troops had taken possession of the school, filled it with wounded soldiers until March or April 1863 and also damaged $1,000 worth of property. That April, the United States Court of Claims investigated these charges. In February 1908, it held a hearing on the claim.[143]

In the case *Trustees of the Ewing Institute of Perryville, Kentucky, v. The United States*, the Federal court determined that the trustees were loyal to the United States and found that the rental value of the property was $270.00. The court wondered why the trustees had waited forty-five years after the battle to present their claim. Attorneys for the school, however, asked the Federal government to reimburse the trustees for the occupation and other damages. They wanted $600.00 in rent, $189.60 for 948 feet of destroyed fencing, $100.00 for repainting and for replacing the faux graining and $200.00 for damage done to windows, shutters, stoves, doors and desks. The government attorney recognized that the building had been occupied and had sustained some damage but asked the government to give the school $100.00 in rent and $100.00 for the "insignificant character of the damages."[144]

On December 5, 1906, U.S. Senate Bill 6831 authorized the payment of $1,000 for the claim. On August 20, 1907, however, the U.S. Treasury Department informed the school that the auditor of the War Department did not have any information about the case. Furthermore, the Treasury Department had no records indicating that the institute was loyal to the Union during the war. Therefore, the Treasury Department returned the petition. On December 28, 1910, an additional claims bill passed the U.S. Senate that allocated $270 for the school, but the claim may never have been paid.[145]

Despite the damages, the institute still found success in the late nineteenth and early twentieth centuries. A successful marketing campaign helped the school retain its solid reputation. One turn-of-the-century newspaper advertisement read, "Parents may feel safe in sending their children to a town so noted for the high moral tone of its inhabitants. Probably no other town in Kentucky is so exempt from the evil influences brought to bear upon young people." Furthermore, another newspaper wrote that the Ewing Institute, with ninety students, "occupies a position as an institution of learning that compares favorably with the best in the State." By 1907, the *Kentucky Gazette* called the school the "leading school in Kentucky."[146]

Despite this favorable press, the school ultimately closed. In the early 1900s, with the increasing availability of public schools, the Ewing Institute shut its doors. From 1915 to 1916, the building housed Perryville High School. By the 1920s, a local casket maker stored his coffins in the structure. The building, now a private residence, was placed on the National Register of Historic Places in 1973.[147]

Like local schools, area churches also met with hardship when, immediately after the battle, wounded soldiers filled the sanctuaries. The Perryville Methodist Church lost $1,200 in damages from burned fencing used for cooking fires, damaged carpet, discolored floors and a missing pulpit. Furthermore, the church's pews were smashed and burned, while several others were dismantled to make coffins for shipping the remains of dead soldiers. The Perryville Presbyterian Church, then located across the street from the Ewing Institute, claimed to have lost nearly $1,000 in damages when Union wounded filled its sanctuary. Damages included discarded pews, smashed shutters, broken windows, unusable stoves, a destroyed chandelier, ruined floors, burned fencing, a removed pulpit and damaged interior plaster. The Christian Church, where dozens of amputations occurred after Federal troops filled the building with Confederate wounded, was also vandalized. The church lost fences and pews, and according to local resident Sue Vandaripe, "a good many died while in there." With churches, businesses and schools damaged, it took the town decades to recover economically.[148]

In addition to the wounded and sick, Perryville residents contended with scores of dead soldiers who lay scattered over hundreds of acres. The Union army buried its own dead in regimental plots, digging the graves near where the men had fallen. One Federal soldier recalled:

The bodies were generally ranged side by side in a trench dug for the purpose, just as they were, with their uniforms crimsoned with blood, wrapped in

"A Sight I Never Wish to See Again"

army blankets for winding sheets, and laid away to rest. In the outskirts of the field where a few had crawled away to die, they were buried singly, and lonely mounds with rudely marked headboards indicated the last resting place of their earthly remains.[149]

The day after the battle, survivors continued to look for wounded comrades and to bury the dead. The sight of the battlefield shocked and saddened them. "The dead bodies of the Rebels lay in every direction," Abraham Knapp of the 10th Wisconsin wrote, "a sight I never wish to see again." Another soldier added, "There was no time for sentiment and the next day in a falling rain our dead comrades were buried." At least twenty-six members of the 38th Indiana were interred in the cornfield on the ridge where they had fallen. These included Alfred and Samuel Kersterson, both of Company I, who were likely brothers. The men were wrapped in blankets and buried in a long trench. Henry Perry wrote, "The burial service held by the Thirty-eighth was very impressive."[150]

When the 3rd Ohio discovered that Bragg was gone, the survivors returned to the hill that overlooked the Bottom House and Doctor's Creek, where they had ferociously battled the Confederates. There, they found several hundred wounded and dead from their regiment and from the 15th Kentucky (Union) Infantry. The injured were carried off to different hospitals, and the dead were buried. Buckeye Colonel John Beatty wrote that the unit had participated in burials before, but past interments were easier because the dead had been strangers. "Now," Beatty wrote, "they are the familiar faces of intimate personal friends, to whom we are indebted for many kindly acts. We hear convulsive sobs, see eyes swollen and streaming with tears [as] our fallen comrades are deposited in their narrow grave."[151]

Two days after the battle, twenty men from the 75th Illinois buried their dead in four two-foot-deep trenches. After wrapping the dead in their blankets, the 75th buried forty-three soldiers. The starkest realization of what occurred on that hot, dry October day came to the members of the 22nd Indiana Infantry. Having lost about 65 percent casualties, they truly knew the cost of Perryville. A former member of the regiment recalled the sense of loss. "On calling the roll at 8 o'clock that night," he wrote, "to nearly every other name in the regiment there was no answer."[152]

Captain William Mitchell of the 1st Wisconsin detailed the burials in his regiment: "The Battle field presented a sad spectacle the poor fellows begging for Gods sake to give them a drink of water." He added:

We Buried all of our Dead But hundreds of Rebels are still in the field together with horses & mules & cattle. The smell is terrible. The Boys from my [company] I helped bury myself. We Buried them about 2 Oclock [sic] in the morning. We wrapt each man in his Blanket and placed their Cartridge Box for a pillow. The Chaplain of the 21ˢᵗ [Wisconsin] was on the field and he kindly assisted and performed the funeral services at the Grave. I could not help the tears trickling down my cheeks as one after another we laid the 4 Brave fellows in the Grave. We have been together for one year, Had [sic] suffered the hardships of a Soldiers [sic] life.[153]

Again, while the Union army buried its own dead, Rebel corpses remained on the field for days after the battle. "Not that [we were] unfeeling or inhuman," one soldier explained, "but it was not [our] business to kill, and then bury traitors." Cincinnati war correspondent Alf Burnett noted, "It is a disgraceful fact that the rebels left their dead unburied. At one spot, in a ravine, they had piled up thirty bodies in one heap, and thrown a lot of cornstalks over them." Burnett added that on the western edge of town some dead Southerners remained unburied for four days. "One," the reporter recalled, "a fine-looking man, with large, black, bushy whiskers, was within a few yards of the toll-gate keeper's house, (himself and family residing there,) who, apparently, was too lazy to dig a grave for the reception of the rebel's body." He added that many Perryville residents—some perhaps shell-shocked—appeared disinterested in the carnage around them. Burnett wrote that "these people seemed to pay no attention to either dead or wounded."[154]

When members of the United States Sanitary Commission complained about the unburied Confederates, Union officers in charge of Perryville ordered Southern sympathizers and impressed slaves to bury them. For two days, these residents dug mass graves and buried hundreds of bodies. Another Union soldier, Private Jonathan McElderry of the 121ˢᵗ Ohio Infantry, stated that five days after the battle the dead still lay on the field. McElderry and others impressed slaves to finish the burials, and two to three wagonloads of corpses were hauled into a nearby cave or sinkhole. Many civilians simply dug holes next to the corpses and pried the bodies into the graves using fence rails.[155]

Beverly D. Williams, a local resident and Federal soldier who was acting quartermaster for Union Brigadier General James S. Jackson, said, "The Confederates took their dead and laid them side by side on the battle field during the night." Again, the Union soldiers refused to bury the dead

Local farmer Henry P. Bottom buried most of the Confederate dead in a mass grave on his property. This 1885 photo shows an elderly Henry Bottom sitting on the beginning of a stone wall that now surrounds the mass grave. Although Bottom tried to identify the Confederate remains, most of the men buried there are listed as "unknown" on the monument that now stands at the site. *Courtesy of the Perryville Battlefield State Historic Site.*

Southerners because Confederate troops had stripped the Northern corpses. William Landrum of the 2nd Ohio Infantry, who fought near the 3rd Ohio and 15th Kentucky, complained, "The Rebels stripped [our] wounded. By the side of every one of our dead men you would see an old pair of shoes and a greasy, filthy pile of clothes…I never hated them till now. I have now a thirst for vengeance: the sight of our men lying scattered over that field has added ten fold to my hatred for them, and I hope the time is not far off when we may have one more chance at them." Since most of these corpses were lying on his farm, Henry Bottom and a number of his field hands and neighbors buried a majority of the Rebel dead.[156]

Other residents assisted with the burials. Joseph Hafley, who lived on Bottom's property as a tenant farmer, claimed that he was "arrested" by Federal authorities and forced to bury the dead, but he "slipped off" to his father's farm, seven miles away. Another local citizen, Nimrod Mullinix, who had a brother and cousins in the Union army at Perryville, worked for "about a week" burying corpses. Burnett wrote that many interments were "accomplished by digging a deep hole beside the corpse, and the diggers, taking a couple of fence rails, would pry the body over and let it fall to the bottom." Because of the dry, rocky soil, some of the graves were only eighteen inches deep.[157]

Some civilian volunteers traveled from other communities to aid with the interments. A professor at the Kentucky Asylum for the Deaf and Dumb (now the Kentucky School for the Deaf) in Danville visited the battlefield after the fight. Shocked by the unburied corpses, the teacher returned the next day with several older students and spent the day with picks and shovels, burying the dead.[158]

The aftermath of the Battle of Perryville struck local residents hard. Their educational and religious institutions were overturned by having wounded soldiers crammed into schools and churches. In addition, most of these buildings were severely damaged, causing severe financial difficulties. These residents also had to contend with unburied Southern corpses, which lay on the battlefield for days after the fight.

Chapter 8
"THE PICTURE OF DESOLATION"

Despite the massive number of casualties and burials undertaken by local civilians, there is only one marked soldier's grave in the town's Hillcrest Cemetery, that of Captain R.E. Ward of the 33rd Alabama Infantry. This regiment was part of Brigadier General S.A.M. Wood's brigade, and they were sent into the fight late in the day. The brigade attacked Union Captain Samuel Harris's six artillery pieces and incurred heavy losses. Of the 380 men in the 33rd Alabama who entered the fight, the regiment suffered 14 killed and 153 wounded. Ward's company, Company B, had 32 men and sustained 23 casualties: 2 soldiers were killed outright, 12 were mortally wounded and 9 others were wounded and later recovered. Among the severely injured was Captain Ward.[159]

The 33rd Alabama faced its baptism of fire at Perryville, and the battle's aftermath was particularly stressful for these fledgling soldiers. One wrote that on the night of the fight, "we carried wheat straw for the wounded to lie upon and water for them in their cedar canteens…Although we were thoroughly tired out…we were up with the wounded boys and assisting the doctors nearly all night. Since it [was frigid] some complained of being cold, their clothing being wet with blood. We wrapped our blankets about them." One of these wounded was likely Captain Ward. G.D. Bush of the 33rd Alabama believed that Ward's wound was fatal. He simply noted, "Capt. Warde shot in the hip verey Dangerous."[160]

Confederate soldier Mathews Preston recalled that Ward knew he would die at Perryville. Afraid that his family would never learn his fate,

Only one marked soldier's grave is located in Perryville's Hillcrest Cemetery. Confederate Captain R.E. Ward of the 33rd Alabama Infantry rests under this simple stone. *Courtesy of the Perryville Battlefield State Historic Site.*

Ward sent his slave, Jesse, to return to Tennessee with the Confederates. Jesse followed his master's orders and, at Knoxville, left the army for Alabama to tell Ward's family about the officer's death. Ward died from his hip wound on October 27, 1862, nineteen days after the battle. It is unknown how he came to be buried in Hillcrest Cemetery in a marked grave. Perhaps the dying Ward stayed with a local family who took pity on the officer and had him buried in a family plot. Or the mortally wounded soldier may have made his own burial arrangements prior to his death. It is also possible that after Jesse returned to Alabama, Ward's family traveled to Perryville, reinterred the body and had the grave marked with the tombstone.[161]

Casualties in Ward's regiment are indicative of what happened to wounded soldiers from Confederate regiments. Sadly, most of these troops

"The Picture of Desolation"

now lie buried in unmarked, forgotten graves. Private Andrew Noblin of the 33rd Alabama's Company G was severely wounded during the battle and was never seen again. Lieutenant Joseph Pellum of Company B was shot though the thigh, resulting in a broken femur. Listed on the casualty rolls as mortally wounded, the officer may have died on the operating table. In Company G, Private Henry McCullough had his knee shattered and died a month later, presumably from complications following an amputation. Several members of the regiment died in hospitals in Harrodsburg, ten miles from the battlefield, and were buried in a mass grave in that town's Springhill Cemetery. These include Captain J.D. McKee of Company D, a soldier from Tuscumbia, Alabama, who died from his wounds nearly three weeks after the battle; and Private Alfred Dewberry of Company C. Others from this regiment were buried farther away. Private Elias Riley of Company B was wounded in the head, placed in an ambulance and joined the Confederate retreat out of Kentucky. As the Rebel army headed south, Riley died on October 18 and was buried somewhere along the road between Bryantsville and Crab Orchard. He, like most of his comrades, rests in an unmarked grave. Other injured soldiers had problems on the march back to Tennessee. R.S. Matthews of the 6th Tennessee, wounded while fighting on the Confederate right flank, retreated to the Volunteer State in an ambulance. "It was a cold journey," Matthews wrote. "One night I was left in the ambulance, and the driver fed and watered his mules in the back part of it. My blanket got wet and froze, and my feet became frostbitten."[162]

At least two members of the 33rd Alabama were wounded at Perryville but died on Northern soil, far from their homes. The wounded Private James L. Pugh of Company D was captured the day after the battle. He died from disease in February 1863 at a Union prisoner of war camp at Alton, Illinois. Alabamian Robert You suffered the same fate. Injured and captured by Federal troops, You died of chronic diarrhea at Alton that same month. These two soldiers survived their wounds only to succumb to disease.

Despite the many post-battle deaths, some survived. Private Robert Phillips of Company B was wounded in the leg, captured and later exchanged. Captain Mason Kinney of Company A was shot "through the bowels" and, despite this dangerous wound, lived to be exchanged in Vicksburg, Mississippi, in November 1862. In Company G, Private L.W. Bigbie was shot in the neck and shoulder and survived the hospitals. Even the regimental commander did not escape the battle unscathed. Colonel

Samuel Adams, the highest-ranking officer in the regiment, was wounded in the foot at Perryville. Adams was one of the lucky ones. He survived.[163]

Like the enslaved Jesse, at least one other slave traveled home to inform the family of his master's demise. While the exact number of slaves who accompanied the Confederates into Kentucky is impossible to ascertain, it is likely that hundreds were forced to follow their masters into the commonwealth during the autumn campaign to operate as cooks and teamsters. One slave owner, Captain John C. Curtwright of Company G, 41st Georgia Infantry, was shot when his regiment attacked several Union artillery batteries. On October 27, Georgian J.M. Leonard vividly informed Curtwright's wife about her husband's death. Leonard wrote, "The ball enter[ed] his right side & passing through, resting on the left side of his spine; not once did he complain of his wound or fall."[164]

Accompanying Curtwright on the battlefield was Berry, the officer's "unusually large" slave. When Curtwright was shot, Berry reputedly exclaimed that the "damn Yankees done shot Marse Jack!" The slave then picked up Curtwright's body and disappeared from the field. Several months later, Berry returned to the Curtwright home in LaGrange, Georgia. He gave Curtwright's widow her husband's watch and sword, telling her that he had given the officer a proper burial and had marked the grave with an inscribed cedar block. Berry told Mrs. Curtwright that since he did not have a coffin, he dug the grave and placed flat stones over the body.

Years later, Curtright's son-in-law hired an attorney to find the captain's grave, but the search failed. In 1919, however, the son-in-law was in Kentucky on business and visited Perryville. A resident recalled the burial and told the son-in-law that when the townspeople interred the Confederates in the mass grave, one slave refused to place his master's body in the pit, informing them that the corpse was a captain and that the burial needed to be "special." The residents paced off ten steps from the large trench, and the slave dug a single grave. The resident told the son-in-law that the inscribed cedar block had been on the field for thirty years, but although the block was gone, he recalled the burial location. The men went to a horse lot, dug down five feet and "found the flat stones and under the stones, the very dark earth, brass buttons and bone fragments." In 1920, the son-in-law had the remains shipped to LaGrange, Georgia, in a mahogany casket. Curtwright was then buried next to his wife in the town's Hillview Cemetery. The captain was finally home. Sadly, Berry's fate is unknown.[165]

"The Picture of Desolation"

While Curtwright's postwar burial garnered attention in LaGrange, the corpse of Union Brigadier General James S. Jackson, the highest-ranking officer killed at Perryville, received the most attention. Jackson, a division commander, was shot twice in the chest on the Union left flank as soon as the fighting started. The general's body was immediately dragged behind the Federal cannon. The next morning, Union officers Samuel Starling and Percival Oldershaw returned to the battlefield to procure Jackson's corpse. There, they "found quite a number of Rebel & Union soldiers, ministering to the wounded and looking at the ground, all animosity had ceased & they were mixing like friends."[166]

A native of Hopkinsville, Kentucky, Brigadier General James S. Jackson led the Union 10th Division at Perryville. Shot twice in the chest, he was killed early in the fight. His body was taken to Louisville and was temporarily interred at Cave Hill Cemetery. Jackson's remains were ultimately moved to Hopkinsville. He was the highest-ranking officer to be killed in the battle. *Courtesy of the Kentucky Historical Society.*

Because of Jackson's rank, Starling and Oldershaw placed the corpse in an ambulance and left for Louisville. Upon reaching Mackville, they "got a large box & a barrel of salt [and] washed him & put him into it." They continued on, stopping briefly in Springfield to rest before moving to Bardstown, where they telegraphed Louisville for a carriage and hearse, which met them at Mount Washington.[167]

The party reached Louisville at 9:00 a.m. on October 11. Jackson's body lay in state at the Galt House Hotel for a day and was then, Starling wrote, "put into a large metallic box (not coffin) & the next day was taken to Christs [*sic*] Church where on entering several Ladies threw wreaths of flowers upon it." The Reverend Jeremiah Talbott gave a eulogy, and then an infantry regiment escorted the body to Cave Hill Cemetery. After a salute was fired, Jackson was placed in a vault. This Federal officer was later reinterred in Hopkinsville, where he had established a law practice and political career prior to the war.[168]

Most of the dead Confederates were buried by Henry P. Bottom. Gathering the bodies in the area where he found the most corpses (where

The Confederate mass grave at the Perryville Battlefield State Historic Site includes a monument and a handful of individual markers. Hundreds of dead Confederates are buried in two pits in the enclosure. Most of the men buried there are unknown casualties. *Courtesy of the Perryville Battlefield State Historic Site.*

"The Picture of Desolation"

Cheatham's division had attacked on the northern end of the battleground), Bottom and his field hands interred several hundred Confederates in two large pits. Bottom also tried to record information about the dead. He detailed names and insignia and made notes about the bodies in a pocket-sized "brown leather-backed notebook." According to Kentucky historian Hambleton Tapp, who examined the now-missing notebook in the 1960s, "In the notebook [Bottom] noted the number of Confederate soldiers found, the places where their corpses were located, and the description of the items found on their bodies. The notebook contains a list of numbers one of which was assigned to each corpse. It also presents a chart of the burying ground and lists the numbers representing the corpses assigned to each pit." Despite Bottom's attempts at identifying the dead, more than four hundred of the soldiers noted on a monument placed over the mass grave are listed as unknown.[169]

According to a Mackville resident, after Bottom buried the bodies, he "cut initials in a shingle and put [the board] over them where they buried them." By 1897, the mass grave was, according to one veteran, "entirely grown up in briers and weeds, and is the picture of desolation." Only one

The inscription on the monument at the Confederate mass grave at the Perryville Battlefield State Historic Site. *Courtesy of the Perryville Battlefield State Historic Site.*

89

grave was marked. Placed by the soldier's wife, it read, "Sam H. Ransom, First Tennessee Regiment, C.S.A., October 8, 1862—age, twenty-seven. 'Our parting is not forever.'" By 1900, the ground was still "grown up in weeds and bushes," and Ransom's grave was still the only marked plot. By this time, however, the stone had broken off at the base. In 1902, the Commonwealth of Kentucky built a stone wall around the mass grave and erected a monument inscribed with verses from Danville native Theodore O'Hara's poem "Bivouac of the Dead." The mass grave is now preserved at the Perryville Battlefield State Historic Site.[170]

Chapter 9
"ENOUGH TO MAKE ANY MAN OPPOSE WAR"

W hen the Confederate army left the battlefield, it hauled many of its wounded to Harrodsburg, ten miles northeast of Perryville. While Perryville residents were unprepared for the appearance of the soldiers, Harrodsburg citizens were ready, having been warned of the battle. Residents cooked food, made bandages and lined up carriages at the edge of town to transport the wounded to makeshift hospitals. When the Southern troops departed town and ultimately left Kentucky, at least 1,700 injured and sick remained in Harrodsburg under the care of the town's 1,700 inhabitants.[171]

Although Harrodsburg mainly contained wounded Rebel soldiers, some Unionists also convalesced in that town. Injured Federal soldiers captured by the Confederates were taken to Harrodsburg with the Southern army and were dropped in area hospitals. In one instance, a hurt Union officer was crowded among Rebel wounded on the porch of a local home. A little girl, upon seeing the Northerner's uniform, cautiously approached and asked him "in low tones" if he was a Union soldier. When the officer replied that he was, the girl later returned with "some delicacies" and "words of sympathy from" her Unionist mother.[172]

Federal forces reached Harrodsburg a few days after the fight and found the town full of wounded Southerners. Although the village had strong Southern sympathies, the Rebel presence—and the fear of catching soldiers' illnesses—persuaded some residents to leave. Two days after the fight, with no residents on the streets, Corporal George Morris of the 81st Indiana wrote, "Not an inhabitant was to be seen, the place was entirely deserted, looking very dismal." Surgeon G.G. Shumard noted that "Perryville and Harrodsburg were already crowded with the wounded, besides these, large numbers of sick and wounded were scattered in houses, barns, stables, sheds, or wherever they could obtain shelter sufficient to protect them from the weather." Private residences in town were filled, and one Harrodsburg woman had twenty-three wounded convalesce in her home.[173]

Many injured Confederates died. Wounded in the hip, C.H. Clark of the 16th Tennessee Infantry was taken to the Harrodsburg courthouse. During his first night there, nine of Clark's wounded comrades passed away. He later wrote that "the moaning and sighing of the wounded and dying that night was heartrending and enough to make any man oppose war." One soldier, Private J.M. Smith of the 9th Tennessee Infantry, died from his wounds in Harrodsburg on January 10, 1863, more than three months after the fight.[174]

Because of the large number of wounded taken to Harrodsburg, many did not receive proper medical attention. Harrodsburg, like other nearby communities, was overwhelmed. Some troops did not receive any attention at all. Maria T. Daviess, author of an early Mercer County history, noted that one soldier who was brought to town was placed "in a solitary room." The wounded man was forgotten and "was never visited again." Daviess explained that when the man was found, he "was too exhausted from wounds and hunger to live." Residents were further saddened when they discovered that he was the younger brother of a minister who had preached in the Harrodsburg Presbyterian Church prior to the war.[175]

The cost of warfare quickly became evident to Harrodsburg's citizens. One witness said that at the Graham Springs Hotel ballroom, there were so many amputations that the severed arms and legs "rose like a pyramid to the floor of the second-story gallery." Most of these surgical procedures took place without the benefit of anesthesia. As one Union surgeon complained, "Of medicines, there were almost none at Harrodsburg." The lack of medicine, little food and the drought all compounded the surgeons' difficulties. Little water was available because wells were empty, and according to one Mercer County historian, horses from the Confederates' supply train drank the "town branch completely dry."[176]

Mary Hunt Afflick was a member of the town's Southern Aid Society, an organization that helped Confederate wounded. "Our lovely town was red with sacrificed blood of wounded heroes brought there from the battle ground of Perryville," Afflick wrote. This ardent Southern sympathizer recalled the difficult mission. "This was no light task in our war-smitten

The Graham Springs Hotel, a Harrodsburg resort, was a Confederate hospital after the battle. One writer remarked that there were so many amputations in the ballroom that the severed arms and legs "rose like a pyramid to the floor of the second-story gallery." The building burned after the Civil War. *Courtesy of Jim Miller.*

land," she wrote, "for it involved self-denial in the home and a great expenditure of time and energy around the war-swept country." The Southern Aid Society, which was initially organized to send funds, food and clothing to Confederates in Northern prison camps, changed its goals when the ill and injured arrived. The society gave the wounded pillows, blankets, clothes, water, food, bandages and "loving words of deathless hope." Indeed, the Southerners under their care had a much easier time than the Confederates who recovered on the stripped Goodnight farm or in other Perryville hospitals.[177]

Descriptions of the town hospitals detail the lack of sanitation. In one packed church were sixty-seven Union soldiers. In addition to wounds received at Perryville, men suffered from typhoid fever, diarrhea and pneumonia. The sick lay on pews and on the floor. Each man had one blanket for warmth and had only "hard bread, beef, and pork" to eat. Despite these conditions, many of the Union troops fared better than the Confederate wounded. While the Federal soldiers had blankets, many of the Rebels lay uncovered on straw.[178]

After touring Harrodsburg's field hospitals, a Union doctor remarked, "In the Methodist Church and College [private school] Hospital were 115 [patients]...They had no bedsacks; all with shirts, pants, and socks; some without coats; a few without blankets; the patients very dirty, their clothing poor." The doctor added that although the hospitals were "well ventilated," they were all filthy.[179]

Once the Confederate forces departed Harrodsburg, leaving their wounded there, the Union army arrived and took charge. On October 25, a member of the Sanitary Commission found 330 wounded and 126 sick Confederate soldiers in Harrodsburg, along with 16 Rebel surgeons, 64 nurses and 24 "servants," likely slaves. Also present were 67 Federals, including 6 wounded and the rest ill, along with 1 surgeon and 8 assistants, "including stewards…and nurses."[180]

To maintain order in town, Federal authorities published orders detailing what was permissible for Union troops, since they were in such proximity to civilians and Rebel prisoners. On November 10, Provost Marshal Captain Joseph P. Black released fourteen orders. First, no one was allowed to sell any type of alcohol to Union or Confederate soldiers, "except upon the prescription of the Medical Director" or an approved surgeon. No one was allowed "to leave this neighborhood without a pass," and the nighttime firing of weapons was prohibited. Because there was a profusion of firearms and other government property left at Perryville and Harrodsburg and scattered between the two towns, all weapons, horses, mules and other supplies were to be turned over to the proper authorities. Selling or buying this property would lead to arrest. Soldiers were not allowed "to enter any private dwelling without invitation unless on duty. No soldier shall insult, misuse, or treat with disrespect any citizen or lady." In addition, to keep the peace in town, "no soldier shall taunt, ridicule, or abuse any Confederate prisoner." Since Harrodsburg contained a significant number of secessionist citizens, everyone in town was to "treat all Federal officers and soldiers with respect" or face arrest. There was also a curfew set at 10:00 p.m., and anyone on the streets after that time was to be arrested. Violation of most of these orders meant imprisonment.[181]

In addition to Harrodsburg, the Confederates left some sick and wounded at the nearby Shaker community of Pleasant Hill. There, on October 11, thousands of Rebel soldiers marched by with their hundreds of wagons and cattle. To feed them, the religious order set up tables and fed an estimated 1,300 Southerners. The next day, the Shakers fed Confederate cavalry, including the famed John Hunt Morgan, whom the Shakers found to be "very polite and courteous and appeared grateful for the hospitalities received." Losses to the community were severe, and the village suffered food

The Shakers at Pleasant Hill in Mercer County fed hundreds of hungry Confederate soldiers during the 1862 Kentucky Campaign. This religious community suffered severe losses. A soldier from Georgia who died there was buried in the Shakers' cemetery. *Courtesy of the Shaker Village at Pleasant Hill.*

shortages, seven hundred burned fence rails and a destroyed cornfield. They also lost 1,350 bushels of corn, nine horses and six wagons. In addition, a Georgia soldier from Kirby Smith's command died at the Shaker village. The Shakers' daily journal notes, "A Company of our brethren followed his remains to our own humble Cemetery where he was decently interred." He remains buried there to this day.[182]

The Harrodsburg hospitals closed in January 1863. Many of the Confederates who died there are now buried in the town's Springhill Cemetery. While most of the Rebels passed away from wounds, a majority of the Union troops who died in Harrodsburg succumbed to disease. Many of these Northerners now rest at the Camp Nelson National Cemetery.[183]

Although most public buildings in Harrodsburg became field hospitals, St. Philips Episcopal Church, built in 1860 and located just off Main Street, was spared. Immediately after the Battle of Perryville, Confederate Major General Leonidas Polk, who was second in command at the battle, went into this church to pray. Polk, who was also an Episcopal bishop, reputedly placed a guard around the church to ensure that it remained a house of worship rather than becoming full of maimed soldiers. While some have argued that the church's dark, stained-glass windows provided too little light for operations, it is unlikely that this alone spared the church. Since soldiers frequently shattered church windows in Perryville and Danville to help ventilate the cramped, foul-smelling hospitals, it is more likely that

Surprisingly, St. Philips Episcopal Church in Harrodsburg was not a hospital after the Battle of Perryville. Confederate General Leonidas Polk, who was also an Episcopal bishop, reputedly placed a guard there to prevent the building from being used as a hospital. Local history contends that the church's stained-glass windows were too dark to enable successful operations, so the building remained unoccupied. *Courtesy of Jim Miller.*

"Enough to Make Any Man Oppose War"

Polk's order saved the sanctuary. The bishop-general likely believed that after the horrific struggle at Perryville, the men needed an undisturbed place to pray.[184]

Just as Perryville and Harrodsburg suffered from the aftermath of Kentucky's largest battle, so, too, did the surrounding communities of Bardstown, Springfield, Lebanon and more. Nearly 2,000 sick and wounded troops were left in Bardstown after the battle, and many others traveled to Louisville for medical care. On October 29, the *Louisville Journal* reported that 1,100 sick and wounded soldiers had been transferred there from Lebanon, and 1,000 more were expected to arrive within the next few weeks. The paper commented, "In the emergency it has been necessary to take possession of additional buildings for hospital purposes, and many others will be seized immediately and converted into apartments for the accommodations of disabled soldiers." Furthermore, New Albany, Indiana, located across the Ohio River from Louisville, had six hospitals for Perryville casualties, including commandeered female colleges. Wounded soldiers from Perryville hospitals started arriving in New Albany on October 18. These hospitals were overwhelmed and made a public plea for clothes, canned and dried fruits, alcohol and bandages. Although it was difficult for troops to make the journey to New Albany or Louisville, one's chances of survival increased with every mile traveled away from Perryville. Aid stations near the battlefield contended with overcrowding, the drought and a lack of medical supplies, and sanitation and overall hospital conditions were much better farther away from the battlefield. While mortality rates likely improved away from Perryville, survival statistics would be skewed because many of the injured in Louisville and New Albany hospitals were walking wounded who suffered from less-severe wounds. Although soldiers did pass away in the Louisville and New Albany hospitals (with 23 dying from October 2 to October 18), the critical patients, who were more likely to die from their injuries, were too hurt to travel. These dangerously wounded remained in Perryville, and many died. In all of these communities, however, scores of citizens were displaced, fences were burned, homes were occupied and livestock was confiscated. It took months for many of these towns to recover.[185]

Although it was safer for wounded troops to reach Louisville or New Albany, the *New Albany Daily Ledger* reported that complaints arose about their hospitals. They contended that surgeons were "criminally negligent in attentions to the sick and wounded placed in their care" and that a "proper diet is not provided the patients." The paper also reported protests about poor sanitation. One patient "begged" a friend, "For God's sake come and take me away from this wretched place, where filth and vermin are overrunning all those too weak to help themselves. I tell you most truly, I am half starved, and if I have to remain in this place another week, I shall surely die." Those who did die at New Albany were Union troops from Indiana, Illinois, Ohio, Kentucky and Michigan. At least one Confederate soldier, G.H. Robins of the 30th Tennessee, passed away in a New Albany hospital.

The *Memphis Daily Appeal* published an alternative view, running an article from Louisville that stated that hundreds of injured were arriving daily and yet the hospitals were "roomy, comfortable, and well attended," with excellent care.[186]

Family members of wounded soldiers also traveled to the Louisville hospitals. Andrew Phillips, who lived in Bainbridge, Ohio, went to "hospital No 10" to visit his nineteen-year-old son, George, who had been wounded while fighting with the 105th Ohio. The hospital contained twenty-four "wounded boys." Andrew wrote his family that George "had some fever," which he supposed was caused by "the excitement of my coming." When Andrew visited, George ate two to three spoonfuls of oyster soup, "a little peach sauce[,] his tin cup of good tea & a piece of toasted bakers bread." George had suffered from severe diarrhea and "sore lungs," which were treated with "a blister plaster on his breast which he did not like very well." He did, however, probably prefer the "number of ladies" who "passed around the room" and "bring in little dainties for the boys."[187]

With no rooms at local taverns because they were full of "drinking dutch & soldiers," Andrew stayed at the camp of the 105th Ohio and slept in a tent "with the boys." After a few days, however, he found a family just two doors down from the hospital who rented a room to him. Although George "was quite weak," he had "a good appetite, [and] ate for breakfast the amount of one good slice of toast one soft boiled egg some peach sauce & a cup of tea" and half of an apple. Although the doctor told Andrew that "he thinks George is better," George died weeks later, on December 19, 1862, probably from his illness.[188]

Although Louisville resources were not strained by the influx of wounded and sick Union soldiers, the city also contended with Confederate prisoners of war from the Battle of Perryville. On October 12, more than 1,300 Rebel POWs arrived and were placed in the "Broadway prison." These troops were ultimately sent to Vicksburg, where they were exchanged.[189]

"Enough to Make Any Man Oppose War"

Because of its proximity to the battlefield, residents in Springfield, Kentucky, cared for the living, dying and the dead. Located sixteen miles west of the battleground, it is likely that Springfield housed mainly Union patients, including men who were trying their best to reach Louisville. Nuns from St. Catharine's, a convent outside of town, traveled to the battlefield, placed wounded in wagons and took them to the convent. The local courthouse was also a hospital for several weeks. Some soldiers died in Springfield, including Private Christian Weinman of the 21st Wisconsin, who expired from a torso wound on November 9. Three days after Weinman's death, one of his comrades, Thomas Allen, wrote Catherine Wright, who was either Weinman's sister or sweetheart, about Christian's demise. Allen recorded:

It is with great sorrow I write to inform you of the death of Christian Weinman. He died in Hospital No. 1 in Springfield, Washington County, Kentucky on the 9th of November. He was shot through the side at the Battle of Perryville and we all thought he was getting better, but he began to be worse and he was out of his mind, but before that, we sent for a priest of the [church] *and he came and the members of the church got him a good coffin and he was buried in the church yard and they got him a good cross made and lettered and he was buried with all the honors of the church so that will be one consolation to know that he is buried as he ought to.*[190]

There were additional deaths in Springfield. At the end of October, an officer in the 50th Ohio Infantry who had been wounded at Perryville died at a relative's home there. This officer, however, had a more formal burial than Christian Weinman. Erastus Winters of that regiment noted that one hundred men from the 50th Ohio took wagons from Lebanon to "bury him with all the honors of war." The troops "were all furnished a pair of white gloves and made quite a nice appearance. When we returned to the house from the graveyard, we were given a fine lunch."[191]

South of Springfield, in Lebanon, the U.S. Sanitary Commission used this town as a distribution point. Dr. Read reported that "a large number of sick" were there, awaiting transportation to Louisville. Hospital railroad cars were created and gathered there and used to transport sick and wounded soldiers northward. By November 14, Lebanon was "a resting place for the sick brought from Perryville and Danville."[192]

West of Springfield, hundreds of wounded and sick soldiers filled Bardstown. Some Confederate sick were left there before the battle, and

Left: Likely wounded while fighting in a cornfield on the Union left flank, Private Christian Weinman died from his injury in Springfield on November 9, a month after the battle. *Courtesy of the Perryville Battlefield State Historic Site.*

Below: Springfield, located about sixteen miles from Perryville, was one of the many area communities where wounded soldiers recovered after the battle. The local courthouse likely held wounded or sick soldiers after the fight. *Courtesy of the Kentucky Historical Society.*

when the Union army arrived and captured 8 of them, a newspaper correspondent wrote, "Many of them will die. They are in a deplorable condition, having been destitute of medicines and nourishment." Ill Union soldiers were also placed there before the battle. Rolin Eleson of the 15th Wisconsin wrote his family that on October 7 "all the sick that could not be active were sent back to Bardstown." Civilians also suffered there. When the Rebel army moved through, it confiscated food, livestock and wagons. One writer noted that "the residents are represented to be in great want." After the battle, Union troops filled homes, businesses and schools. St. Joseph College, a Catholic school, housed 310 patients, including 60 Rebels. One chronicler of the occupation wrote that the Union and Confederate troops "drank and quarreled with one another, rode roughshod over all the hospital regulations, stole the college poultry and vegetables and invaded the private apartments of the fathers, the officers being unable to control them. A sigh of relief was breathed by the Jesuits when on October 17 some sixty or seventy of these undisciplined guests received their discharge from the hospital."[193]

St. Joseph College in Bardstown contained several hundred sick soldiers after the Battle of Perryville. The Catholic priests in charge of the school had difficulty maintaining order, as recovering troops "drank and quarreled with one another, rode roughshod over all the hospital regulations, stole the college poultry and vegetables and invaded the private apartments of the fathers, the officers being unable to control them." *Courtesy of the Kentucky Historical Society.*

Many wounded soldiers who were left in these communities never made it home. Dr. Jefferson J. Polk remarked that "hundreds of the wounded died every week," and Dr. Read recorded that the mortality rate "has been large." Because of disease and complications caused by drought and crowded, unsanitary hospitals, many died. From October 9, 1862, until December 24, there were post-battle deaths every day. While no one died on Christmas Eve, the deaths continued the following day. Although the Perryville hospitals closed on March 23, 1863, the last known recorded death directly related to the battle was on June 30, 1863, more than eight months after the fight.[194]

Many troops were appreciative of the civilians who nursed the sick and wounded. Federal soldier S.K. Crawford wrote, "It has never been my good fortune to visit that Perryville locality in these intervening years, but I have often wished to thank the people…for their many kind acts. We appreciated their aid in the day of our extremity."[195]

Chapter 10
"HER GRIEF WAS HEART-RENDING"

While Harrodsburg residents helped hundreds of wounded and sick Confederates, the Unionist community of Danville, located ten miles east of Perryville, dealt with thousands of ill and injured Federal troops. Of the communities located beyond Perryville, perhaps none suffered as much as Danville, which became inundated with patients who filled the courthouse, churches, schools, businesses and other institutions. There had, however, been warning of the chaos that descended upon Danville during the autumn campaign. As early as September 27, several buildings on the Centre College campus, adjacent to downtown, had been commandeered by Confederate troops and converted into field hospitals for sick men who could no longer march.[196]

Elizabeth Patterson, the Unionist wife of a Centre College mathematics professor, remembered the Confederate presence. She wrote, "At night, the college campus would be lighted up by cheerful campfires around which the soldiers at the hospital would gather, sitting upon logs of firewood and singing rebellious songs, such as 'Dixie.'"[197]

On October 13, five days after the battle, the Federal army marched into Danville, where throngs of Unionist citizens warmly greeted it. Upon reaching the college campus, the Northern troops evicted the ill Southerners, sending most of them to Danville's First Baptist Church. Centre buildings were again filled with the wounded and sick, but this time they were Northern patients.

Union surgeon G.G. Shumard arrived in Danville three days later, where he "found about fifteen hundred sick, without shelter, most of them remaining

Left: Many buildings in downtown Danville became hospitals after the battle. The Episcopal church (left) and the First Presbyterian Church (far right) were both full of wounded and sick soldiers. *Courtesy of Centre College.*

Below: This image from *Harper's Weekly* depicts the 9th Indiana Infantry marching into Danville after the Battle of Perryville. The church on the left, Trinity Episcopal, and many of the buildings along Main Street became hospitals after the battle. *Courtesy of the Kentucky Historical Society.*

where they had fallen from the ranks of the army as it marched through the town. In two days the number of sick at this point was increased to two thousand five hundred." When the Union army pursued the Confederates out of the commonwealth, many of the sick were deposited in Danville. Within the next few days, churches, homes and public buildings became hospitals for thousands of patients. Dr. E.W. Banks of Indiana noted, "Our army returning through Danville, left upon the streets four thousand sick and wounded soldiers. They were placed in churches, colleges, houses, blacksmith shops, stables, in fact, Danville was one great hospital."[198]

At the end of October, Danville resident Fanny Bell wrote her aunt: "We have three thousand five hundred Federal soldiers and something over a hundred confederates [*sic*] in town. You can imagine what Danville is with that much sickness. The court house, seminary buildings, every church and unoccupied house, private dwellings and all are full to overflowing." As Danville had approximately five thousand residents in 1862, the number of Union and Confederate troops nearly doubled the population of the town and strained the city's resources.[199]

Dr. A.N. Read was also worried about conditions in Danville. After touring hospitals in Mackville and Perryville, Read found "the wants of the sick [in Danville] as urgent as those of the wounded at Perryville. The Courthouse was literally packed."[200]

The Centre College buildings were also full of sick and wounded troops.

Rebuilt after a fire destroyed many buildings in Danville, the Boyle County Courthouse was reopened shortly before the Battle of Perryville. After the fight, the building became crammed with wounded and sick troops. *Courtesy of the Kentucky Historical Society.*

Centre professor Ormond Beatty's chemistry laboratory in Old Centre was converted into a postmortem examination room and was also likely an operating room. After the war, Beatty became president of the college. *Courtesy of Centre College.*

Union authorities estimated that "Old Centre," the main college building, could hold 150 patients, and it was soon at capacity. "I saw the poor, sickly wounded soldiers all over the building," former student E.W.C. Humphrey commented, "and the use which they made of the building was about as severe as it could have been." A downstairs chemistry lab became an operating room, and some students had to go through it on their way to class. Student A.B. Nelson later noted that "we had to pass through a room occupied by one of the Federal surgeons—or several of them, as a dead-house or post mortem room...I have seen more than one post mortem examination held in this room while I was passing through."[201]

Many patients died. Nelson testified, "I have seen soldiers—the bodies of soldiers taken out of there in the hearse for burial; I would see them every day or two." Another former student remarked that Old Centre was full of "some very sick soldiers; plenty of them that died." Burials were so frequent that troops remained on campus for the sole purpose of interring the dead.[202]

"Her Grief Was Heart-Rending"

Centre College's main building was used by Union and Confederate troops as a hospital before and after the battle. The building was heavily damaged by the occupation. *Courtesy of Centre College.*

The Union army occupied campus until late June 1863, more than eight months after the Battle of Perryville. Old Centre was left in shambles, and the two literary society libraries located in the upstairs of the building were also heavily damaged. Desks and chairs were destroyed, windows were smashed, plaster was broken and the chemistry lab was ruined. While few classes were cancelled on campus—they were held elsewhere—recitations did not resume in Old Centre until September 1863, nearly one year after the battle.[203]

Area churches were some of the first structures to be turned over to the suffering troops, and no denomination was spared. Mary Harris, a housekeeper who attended the First Baptist Church, related that "the churches were filled as rapidly as they could bring them; I couldn't say which church was filled first." Dr. Read noted that one contained seventy-eight patients who suffered from typhoid fever, diarrhea and pneumonia. Most of the men had only the clothes on their backs, and many had no blankets. Three small kettles were used to cook for all of these troops.[204]

In the Methodist church, Read remarked, the men shared blankets as they lay on the pews or on the straw-covered floor of the sanctuary.

When he visited the Episcopal church, he found the circumstances to be similarly inadequate. Three kettles and three frying pans cooked meals for the 161 patients housed there.[205] The Episcopal church contained both Union and Confederate soldiers, and damage to the structure was severe. Outside fencing was destroyed, pews were "defaced" when blankets were tacked between the pews to make beds, doors were removed, lights were broken, prayer books were ruined, the carpet was destroyed and, according to one witness, "the walls were written over and blackened considerably." Members were further saddened because the Episcopal church had recently been rebuilt after a fire consumed the original structure in February 1860. One resident, Mrs. H.L. Newlin, stated, "I know some of the members were dreadfully distressed to think their church was being used for a hospital when they had just gotten it fixed up."[206]

Mary Harris's First Baptist Church, described by her as "a very nice comfortable building," became full of sick and wounded Union soldiers. Although the pews were initially used as beds, the soldiers eventually removed them when cots became available, a rare luxury for convalescents in Danville. Anna Bowman, who was "matron of the Deaf and Dumb Institution," lived nearby. She later noted, "I remember seeing them lying on the floor and on benches, with the bandages on their arms and legs and heads." Several residents testified that the First Baptist Church was the last house of worship to be vacated by the soldiers. According to teacher Henrietta Wilson, the church was occupied a day or two after the battle and was in use as a hospital until the late spring or early summer of 1863. The occupation likely lasted for more than eight months.[207]

When the troops departed, the church was left in shambles. Housekeeper E.E. Akin took milk to patients in several Danville churches. She later related that the building was in "pretty bad" shape. "The windows [were] broken," she stated, "fences all gone, front and back, too. It was badly knocked up." In addition, the floor "looked dirty and bad," and the walls were "badly scarred." Mary Harris found the church "in a very dilapidated condition." Walls and pews were "defaced," pews were split for kindling and other benches were removed. "I know there was cooking done in the house," Harris said. The pulpit, used as a table to hold medicines, was ruined, and the fencing around the church was burned for firewood. In the early 1900s, the church attempted to get $1,900 in damages and rental fees by filing a war claim against the Federal government, but in August 1907, that claim was rejected. By that time, however, the original building was gone; fifteen or

"Her Grief Was Heart-Rending"

Danville's First Presbyterian Church was a hospital after the Battle of Perryville. Witnesses testified that it was full of sick soldiers. Heavily damaged after the occupation, G.W. Welsh said that "a great many people [were] afraid to attend services at that church until it was scraped and painted and varnished and cleaned" because they feared catching illnesses. *Courtesy of the Presbyterian Church of Danville.*

twenty years after the Battle of Perryville, the church burned to the ground. In addition, the Presbyterian Church was "mutilated" after the occupation, and several others suffered similarly.[208]

Hardly any religious institution was spared. The Danville Presbyterian Theological Seminary, which opened in 1853, was housed in a large brick building that had served as the first statehouse of Kentucky. The commonwealth's first constitution was adopted in this building, but after Perryville's battle, this and other buildings on the seminary's campus became full of wounded and sick soldiers. Mary Harris, who nursed the injured and wrote letters home for many of the men, noted, "I was in that building every day, and I bathed the brow of many a soldier in there, both Federal and Confederate."[209]

Although both sides were crammed in the structure, they did not co-mingle. Union troops were placed in the west side of the building, while the Southerners were housed in the eastern end. Danville tailor Abraham Barker supposed that "they had them in different sides to keep them, I reckon, from fighting." Dr. Read reported that all of the soldiers on the seminary campus "were all badly wounded," while Mary Harris testified that "they were all to pieces—some of them shot to pieces, some of them with shell and some with bullets; there were amputations." Despite the severity of the wounds, the care was outstanding. Read believed that of all the Danville hospitals, including the courthouse and most churches, the seminary was "the best of the series" because all the other hospitals were "far too much crowded." The seminary, however, was badly damaged by the occupation, with destroyed wallpaper, plaster, windows, doors and floors. Reportedly the last Danville hospital to be cleared of soldiers, the seminary was unable to use any of the buildings for nearly two years. Damages were estimated at $5,000.[210]

In all churches and hospitals, death rates were high. Read reported that one unnamed church contained "65 men today, last night 128." High mortality was further noted by Elizabeth Patterson, who wrote, "The long rows of soldiers' graves in the beautiful cemetery of Danville attest the mortality at that time of suffering." At least 100 of the more than 400 Union soldiers buried in the national cemetery at Danville's Bellevue Cemetery died of illnesses contracted during the Perryville Campaign, while at least another 30 died of wounds received in the battle.[211]

As the churches and the Centre campus became crowded, local businesses and homes became hospitals. In one downtown carriage shop, more than two hundred Federal troops were placed on the straw-covered floor. When the surgeons toured the Jackson House, a private residence, they found eighty sick men in eight eighteen- by eighteen-foot rooms. Thanks to the supervising surgeon, Read remarked proudly, "no part of the building was soiled or defaced."[212]

While a variety of diseases plagued the soldiers, Shumard stated that most of the sick in Danville were ill from typhoid fever. The soldiers also suffered from pneumonia, measles and dysentery. Many of the illnesses were passed on to citizens. Fanny Bell informed her aunt, "The sickness is not now confined to the soldiers. Almost every family has some [cases], not all dangerous, but complaining with the dreadful camp disease." So great was the outbreak of typhoid, Patterson related, that "not a day passed without one or more funerals. Several ladies of prominent families died from this fever." As illnesses raged through the community, doctors from the Centre College hospital advised nearby residents to keep their front doors and windows closed and to stay in the backs of their homes to avoid disease.[213]

Sadly, measles claimed the lives of two relatives who served in the same regiment. Private Marion Clemens and Private Phillip Clemens, brothers born in Alabama, served in Company K of the Union's 15th Kentucky Infantry Regiment. At Perryville, the 15th Kentucky defended a hill on the Union right flank, immediately above the home of Henry P. Bottom. Their regiment endured consecutive Confederate attacks. During the fighting, the 500 members of the unit sustained 62 killed, 136 wounded and 5 missing. In addition to these battlefield casualties, the regiment also lost men to sickness. While Marion and Phillip Clemens survived the fighting at Perryville, both

The grave of Marion Clemens, Bellevue Cemetery, Danville. Marion and Philip Clemens, brothers who were members of the 15th Kentucky Union Infantry Regiment, died in Danville of measles on December 7, 1862, and were buried in the National Cemetery portion of Bellevue Cemetery. *Courtesy of the author.*

The grave of Philip Clemens. *Courtesy of the author.*

men died of measles on December 7, 1862, nearly two months after the battle. Both men were buried in Bellevue Cemetery.[214]

In addition to enlisted soldiers dying from illnesses, the 15th Kentucky also lost its colonel, Curran Pope, to sickness. Pope, a Louisville native and West Point graduate, had been an engineer and long-term clerk of the Jefferson County Court before he raised the 15th Kentucky Infantry. At Perryville, Pope's horse was killed out from under him. He was then shot in the shoulder, or what he called "the fleshy part of my arm." The colonel initially remained with his regiment to chase the Confederates out of Kentucky, but after a few days, he realized that he needed medical attention. Pope found his way to the Danville home of a family cousin, the Reverend Edward P. Humphrey. Although Pope's wound showed improvement, on November 5, he died of typhoid fever at the Humphrey home. The officer was buried in Louisville's Cave Hill Cemetery. Union Major General William T. Sherman told Pope's widow, "Among all the men I have ever met in the progress of this unnatural war, I cannot recall one in whose every act and expression was so manifest the good and true man; one who so filled the type of the Kentucky gentleman." Disease claimed this promising officer and many other soldiers.[215]

Caregivers also succumbed to sickness. After the battle, a young soldier named Charles W. Orcutt of the 87th Indiana Infantry Regiment worked as a nurse in one of the Centre College buildings. Elizabeth Patterson fondly remembered Orcutt. "The nurse who was in attendance and waited upon me that day was a young man named Orcutt," she wrote, "who appeared to be the very embodiment of physical health and strength." Furthermore, Patterson recalled, the doctors at the college hospital depended on Orcutt because of his strength and dependability. One night, while Patterson's husband Robert was at the college, Elizabeth heard "the most fearful screams, evidently proceeding from one of the rooms in the college building." When Robert returned, he told her that

> *the agonizing cries were those of Orcutt—the nurse—who had been seized with neuralgia of the heart. The physicians said there was no hope; he was dying; they could do nothing…Poor fellow! He had helped save others, but he himself must die. He breathed his last the next morning. His young wife arrived the day after his death. Her grief was heart-rending. They buried him* [in Bellevue Cemetery] *with military honors.*[216]

"Her Grief Was Heart-Rending"

A soldier who worked as a nurse in the Centre College hospitals, Charles Orcutt died of "neuralgia of the heart." According to Elizabeth Patterson, a professor's wife, "His young wife arrived the day after his death. Her grief was heart-rending. They buried him [in Bellevue Cemetery] with military honors." *Courtesy of the author.*

The civilian caregivers who died of illnesses contracted from the soldiers remain the forgotten casualties of the battle. Centre College's president, Lewis Warner Green, was one of these who paid the ultimate sacrifice for helping the sick. Green, a Danville native and son of a prominent family, was Centre's first graduate. After attending Princeton Theological Seminary, he became a Presbyterian minister and served as president of Hampden-Sydney College in Virginia and Transylvania University in Lexington, Kentucky, before assuming the helm of Centre College. During the nineteenth century, Green was one of the Bluegrass State's preeminent intellectuals. While nursing sick Northern soldiers at the college, Green contracted an illness, suffered for five days and died on May 26, 1863, more than seven months after the battle. Although he did not perish on the battlefield, Green's death is inexorably linked to the aftermath of the Battle of Perryville.[217]

Caregivers continually exhibited fortitude in the face of mass hardships. Many Danville residents nursed the sick and wounded soldiers, and citizens frequently took food and other items to the hospitals. Professor Jacob Cooper recalled Elizabeth Moore, who helped injured troops on the Perryville battlefield before she returned home to Danville to aid convalescents in the college hospital. "I have known and loved many good people," Cooper

One of Kentucky's preeminent nineteenth-century intellectuals, Centre College President Lewis Warner Green died from an illness that he reputedly contracted while helping sick Union soldiers after the Battle of Perryville. Green is buried in Danville's Bellevue Cemetery. *Courtesy of Centre College.*

wrote. "I have seen many who were unselfish, self-sacrificing, indefatigable in doing good, but I have never known anyone who excelled Mrs. Moore. No language can adequately express her goodness." Moore let sick soldiers recover in her home, and at least one died there. She also visited the Centre hospitals each day, "carrying necessaries and delicacies for the sick." She was also known for her bravery. Later in the war, when Confederate cavalry stole one of her horses, Moore walked downtown, found the horse and refused to let go of the bridle until the perplexed Rebel rider returned it to her. Finally, thanks to the intervention "of a prominent citizen," she returned home with the mount.[218]

For sick and wounded soldiers in Danville, there were several factors that compounded the suffering, including a lack of medical supplies and the scarcity of food and water. In Danville, one army surgeon paid one dollar "from his own pocket for the only ounce of opium in town." There was also little food to ease hunger pangs felt by the ailing troops. Agents of the Sanitary Commission found that "the only food obtainable for the sick, was the army ration for well men—hard bread, bacon and fresh beef, coffee and sugar. Milk, eggs, butter, chickens, vegetables, etc., are not to be had at any price." A final difficulty was the lack of water. As thirsty soldiers drank from brackish pools, the number of sick increased dramatically. When troops convalesced in Danville, water had to be hauled into town from more than a mile away. As there were thousands of patients in Danville, this must have been hundreds of gallons—and dozens of trips to the water source—each day.[219]

Dr. Read's difficulty in making soup for the patients in the county courthouse was illustrative of these problems. At first it seemed to be an impossible task, for there was no beef, no water ("the wells were all dry") and no kettles (according to Read, they had all been taken by the Confederates). Finally, after more than five hours of scrounging, Read had two thirty-two-gallon kettles of soup boiling on the courthouse lawn.[220]

While most Danville institutions were occupied as hospitals and severely damaged, the quick thinking of one administrator saved the Kentucky Asylum for the Deaf and Dumb, now known as the Kentucky School for the Deaf. During the Perryville Campaign, Confederate officers tried three times to convert the spacious buildings on the deaf school's campus into hospitals; twice they were rebuffed, and when the Rebels appeared a third time, the school's superintendent, J.A. Jacobs, "informed the Confederate Medical Director that if the buildings were taken he together with all the

Built in 1852, the old chapel at the Kentucky School for the Deaf is no longer standing. These buildings were not used as hospitals because the superintendent of the school threatened to leave the deaf students under the care of military surgeons. *Courtesy of the Jacobs Hall Museum, Kentucky School for the Deaf.*

other school officers, would at once abandon them, leaving the deaf children to the care of the Confederate officers who would be held responsible for them. This firm stand...averted the calamity." Although deaf students had helped with burials, their quarters would be spared from becoming hospital rooms. Confederate doctors would rather find other quarters than try to handle dozens of hearing-impaired students.[221]

Eventually, the number of patients in Danville decreased. By November 12, due to deaths and recovery, there were 925 patients in town, but the hospitals would remain in use for more than four more months. It was not until February 27, 1863, that soldiers left the Centre College buildings. Although the sick were gone, Union authorities used the structures as administrative headquarters for several more weeks. In March, the Centre College faculty minutes recorded that on the fourteenth, "the building is restored to the college authorities, after twenty days of occupation by the Confederates, and five months, less two days, by the U.S. forces." Some wounded and sick remained in Danville for several more months. Scores of men never made it home.[222]

Chapter 11
"THE BEST OF
SOLDIERS"

Another casualty of the Battle of Perryville and its aftermath was Union morale in the Army of the Ohio. After the fight, soldiers on both sides were exhausted from the arduous campaign. Having marched hundreds of miles in the dust of drought-ravaged Kentucky, many of the troops were exhausted, in ill health and ready to go home. Many in the 8th Kentucky Union Infantry regiment decided to do just that, and their experiences illustrate how Union morale dropped despite the Federals' success in chasing the Rebels from the Bluegrass State.[223]

Organized by an Estill County attorney, Colonel Sidney Barnes, the 8th Kentucky operated near Nashville before missing the Battle of Shiloh in April 1862. Following that battle, the regiment spent the next several months marching and countermarching through middle Tennessee, chasing Confederate cavalry. These maneuvers became more intense as Bragg and Kirby Smith invaded Kentucky. The 8th joined the pursuit, and upon crossing the Kentucky state line, "the boys gave three lusty cheers." Although they were happy to be back in the commonwealth, the campaign severely tested the untried regiment. The men were allocated half rations and were forbidden to forage because the officers feared it would set a "bad example" if these Kentuckians stripped food from home state civilians. Furthermore, the drought accentuated their difficulties. "We halted half an hour at a filthy pond," their regimental historian wrote, "where the men were allowed to fill their canteens with what they called 'mule soup,' as there were several dead carcasses lying putrefied in the water, probably intentionally placed there by the armed 'Southern gentlemen.'" Finally, on September 25, the ragged and exhausted men reached Louisville.[224]

The 8th Kentucky advanced with Buell's army but was not engaged at Perryville. Following the fight, additional rough marching lay ahead of the men as they pursued Bragg. By October 19, Barnes's regiment was in Crab Orchard. They were exhausted, had no tents and little camp equipment, consumed poor rations and had not been paid for six months. Morale plummeted. Barnes asked his officers to keep the troops quiet, but disharmony reigned. The men, near their homes, wanted to return to Estill and other nearby counties. To ease tensions, the colonel requested furloughs for the married men in the regiment, but their corps commander, fellow Kentuckian Major General Thomas L. Crittenden, denied the request. Crittenden's refusal enhanced the grumbling in the ranks because many of the officers' wives, including Barnes's wife, Elizabeth, were visiting their husbands. Not even back pay, which arrived on November 4, could squelch the complaints. That night, with greenbacks in their pockets, at least fifty men deserted. Many more would follow.[225]

Anger over officers' privileges, homesickness, late pay, poor rations and simple exhaustion were not the only reasons that the men wanted to return home. During the Perryville Campaign, Confederate troops had operated throughout eastern Kentucky. Therefore, the men wanted to check on their families, farms and firesides. Confederate cavalry, for example, camped at a resort that Barnes owned at Estill Springs. The Rebel horsemen consumed food and livestock, and Barnes expressed irritation that the Southerners "camped and hitched [their] horses in my yard to my shrubbery." Confederates also took apples from Barnes's orchard and peeled them on the family's porch. When Elizabeth Barnes walked by the Rebels, they threw the peels at her feet. One of her pro-Confederate relatives stayed at the property to try to minimize damages.[226]

In proximity to their homes and with the campaign over, scores of men in the 8th Kentucky left the army without permission. By November, despite the number of troops missing from the ranks, the regiment had returned to middle Tennessee. Sickness and desertions diminished the regiment to fewer than three hundred men. A month later, on December 10, the *Frankfort Daily Commonwealth* issued an appeal for absent soldiers to return to the unit. Since the notice did not threaten punishments for those who were absent without leave, it is evident that the Union high command was not surprised that these AWOL soldiers had returned to their nearby homes once Kentucky was safe from Confederate occupation. Instead, only the men who were still absent on January 8, 1863, would be punished as deserters. The high number of soldiers absent without leave illustrates the strain put on the regiment during the Perryville Campaign. Most of the men, however, ultimately returned, and several of the AWOL Kentuckians were eventually killed in battle. Heavily engaged at the Battles of Stones River and Chickamauga, the regiment later earned acclaim at Lookout Mountain by being the first to plant its flag on the cliffs of the mountain.[227]

The notice published in the *Frankfort Daily Commonwealth* shows the strain that the Perryville Campaign placed on the inexperienced regiment. Many of the absent soldiers, however, returned to the unit and fought with distinction in several of the largest battles in the Western Theater. By the Battle of Lookout Mountain, these Kentuckians were veterans. Absences in late 1862 were caused by the soldiers' proximity to home, a fear of Confederate depredations in eastern Kentucky, exhaustion, poor rations and frustration about officers' privileges. Most of the men returned to fight, and when they furled their banner for the last time, they were, the regimental historian noted, "the best of soldiers."

Sadly, many of the best soldiers were left dead and wounded on the hills outside of Perryville. In addition, the physical damage to farms and businesses took months to repair, while the constant marching of troops throughout the area after the battle continued to cause damages. Union soldier Lyman Widney remarked that property continued to be obliterated. The Federals pursued Bragg eastward through Danville and to Crab Orchard before Widney's regiment returned through Perryville. "The country we traversed from Crab Orchard to Perryville displayed the terrible ravages of war," Widney wrote. "Our army had followed Bragg's over it, and now we had passed back again, and what Bragg spared or we spared in our advance we demolished on our return. Fences gone, orchards cut down, fields obliterated, and the very sod trampled into dust. Deserted houses in the midst of this desolate plain marked the places where three weeks before productive farms supplied peaceful homes with a plentiful subsistence." Widney added, "Near Perryville the scene was more deplorable. The field was not strewn with human bodies as 10 days before, but long lines of freshly-turned clay masked the trenches where Confederate dead had been heaped one upon the other and so scantily covered that a hand or a foot might be seen protruding...Our own dead had been buried in separate graves and marked by comrades. The carcasses of faithful horses were still there."[228]

As Widney relates, the impact of the aftermath of the Battle of Perryville was immense and lasted for an extended period. The battle, and the damages, took a toll on the village, which became economically stagnant. William L. Linney, for example, whose family moved to Perryville in 1866, stated, "Everything in the place looked old. There wasn't a modern improvement in [town]." He added, "Of course the end of the Civil War had left its mark on the town, and everywhere there were some undesirable characters." This led to a breakdown in the local justice system, and many turned to vigilantism.[229]

The aftermath overwhelmed and horrified residents of multiple communities. These citizens, who became caregivers, contended with patients for months. This was dangerous work, for civilians died from diseases passed on by the troops. Within these communities, as schools were occupied, local educational systems were left in shambles. Centre College, the Kentucky School for the Deaf, the Ewing Institute and countless other private academies delayed classes and lost thousands of dollars in tuition. In addition, the religious life of these communities was overturned as churches became hospitals and were damaged by the soldiers. Furthermore, the local governments in all of these communities were negatively impacted as courthouses became hospitals, the county court proceedings were delayed and magistrates—like justice of the peace Henry P. Bottom—contended with casualties and rebuilt destroyed farms. The Boyle County Circuit Court, for example, held its February 1863 term "in the large room upon the second floor of C.W. Mitchell's building," which had previously been a furniture storeroom.[230] The aftermath also showed Kentuckians—many of whom remained sitting on the fence safe from major battles—that the war could reach into the Bluegrass State and overturn their lives. They now knew that a large battle in a small community of three hundred inhabitants had a large footprint, impacting communities as far away as southern Indiana. Wounded Confederate troops also traveled into Tennessee upon Bragg's retreat, and some soldiers recovered from their wounds even farther south. Confederate Captain William Carnes, for example, went to Macon, Georgia, "to receive medical treatment" for an injury and illness. Civilians who helped these wounded men were thereby affected by Perryville's aftermath.[231]

The aftermath also affected the armies. In addition to the losses in men, horses and supplies, Perryville showcased the Army of the Ohio's lack of preparedness for casualties. Buell's order limiting one ambulance per brigade caused suffering and illustrated that some commanders' thinking revolved more around tactics and strategy than the general care of their men. However, Buell's failure to prepare enabled the United States Sanitary Commission to shine and showed that organization's importance in helping wounded and sick troops.

Burials on the field displayed animosity between the opposing sides. Since Confederate troops scoured bodies for clothes and weapons, Union soldiers refused to bury their enemies, thereby allowing buzzards, crows and hogs to cover the field. This added to the unsanitary conditions and accentuated civilians' involvement with the aftermath, as they were forced to bury most of the Southern dead. The aftermath also detailed how external factors—notably the drought—severely impacted post-battle operations, including surgery and disease. Doctors' hands and surgical tools could not be properly washed, and illness spread as soldiers drank from stagnant ponds. The loss in manpower from deaths and disability from disease was preventable but, in many cases, was caused by a lack of water.

For many Union soldiers, Perryville was their baptism of fire. It was also the first time that these troops saw mass suffering. In addition to being shocked by the intensity of the fight, they were also saddened by the suffering of the wounded and fearful of the swine. The end of the campaign disillusioned both Union and Confederate troops. Federal soldiers were angry at Buell for not bagging Bragg's army and were disgusted by his inability to prepare properly for the wounded. The Confederates were similarly disillusioned at Bragg's failures and with Kentuckians' refusal to join the Confederate army.

As Kentucky was a border state, the proximity of Perryville to states that supplied men to both armies allowed relatives of casualties to visit the field to find their dead and wounded family members. Because of Perryville's location near Tennessee, Ohio, Indiana, Illinois, Wisconsin and other states, civilian visitation to the battlefield played a major role in the aftermath. Sarah Coleman from Wisconsin, Mrs. Hamilton from Lexington, Joshua Barbee from Danville, Andrew Phillips from Ohio and many, many more found wounded relatives and exhumed the dead. Their direct experiences—which they were unable to have with battles fought elsewhere, farther from home—spread the effect of the aftermath to neighboring states, thereby increasing Perryville's already large footprint. No other Western Theater battlefield had this impact, for no other massive fight was held in such proximity to the homes of soldiers both North and South.

Perhaps the cruelty of the aftermath was best described by Stewart B. Nixon, a soldier in the 52nd Ohio Infantry Regiment. Nixon's most striking remembrance was not about generals like James Jackson, who were given a

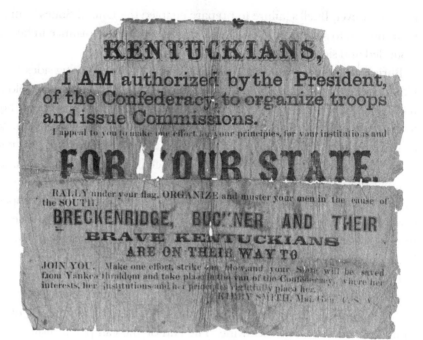

Confederate General Edmund Kirby Smith's recruiting broadside. When the Confederate armies entered Kentucky in the summer of 1862, one of their goals was to recruit Kentuckians. This objective failed, and after the campaign, Bragg was bitter about Kentuckians' failure to rally to the Rebel standard. *Courtesy of the Kentucky Historical Society.*

hero's burial, or the scores of Confederate dead interred by local civilians. Instead, Nixon recalled how the smallest soldiers suffered:

> *Passing a building where the enemy had left their wounded, we were attracted by the cry of a rebel drummer boy. He was in the delirium of death. Some one had leaned a broad plank against the side of the building where he lay, to keep the drip from the eaves of the house from falling in his face, for it was raining as it always did after a battle. I shall never forget that sweet, childish voice; he said in his delirium, "mother, dear mother, why don't you come and take me home?" That mother did not come. She lived far away, perhaps in some beautiful home in the sunny south. She never saw her boy again, for as we returned, his form was still, his childish voice was hushed in death and we thought may it not be that the angels did come and take him to the home above.*[232]

NOTES

CHAPTER 1

1. New Albany editorial reprinted in *Memphis Daily Appeal*, November 15, 1862.

2. Thomas L. Connelly, *Army of the Heartland: The Army of Tennessee, 1861–1862* (Baton Rouge: Louisiana State University Press, 1967), 188, 190, 191; Earl J. Hess, *Banners to the Breeze: The Kentucky Campaign, Corinth, and Stones River* (Lincoln: University of Nebraska Press, 2000), 7; Larry J. Daniel, *Days of Glory: The Army of the Cumberland, 1861–1865* (Baton Rouge: Louisiana State University Press, 2005), 86; Thomas L. Connelly, *Civil War Tennessee* (Knoxville: University of Tennessee Press, 1979), 8–9, 11; James Lee McDonough, *War in Kentucky: From Shiloh to Perryville* (Knoxville: University of Tennessee Press, 1994), 39–40.

3. For the Battle of Richmond, see D. Warren Lambert, *When the Ripe Pears Fell: The Battle of Richmond, Kentucky* (Richmond, KY: Madison County Historical Society, 1999); and McDonough, *War in Kentucky*, 129–46.

4. For the Battle of Munfordville, see McDonough, *War in Kentucky*, 160–81; Stuart W. Sanders, "Honor and Ego at Munfordville," *Civil War* (August 1997): 19–25.

5. Ira S. Owens, *Greene County in the War, Being a History of the Seventy Fourth Regiment* (Xenia, OH: Torchlight Job Rooms, 1872), 166; "dead mule" quoted in Lowell H. Harrison, "Death on a Dry River," *Civil War Times Illustrated* 18 (May 1979): 9.

6. For information about the fight at Peter's Hill, see Kenneth W. Noe, *Perryville: This Grand Havoc of Battle* (Lexington: University Press of Kentucky, 2001), 145–56; McDonough, *War in Kentucky*, 220–23.

7. Porter quote from U.S. War Department, *The War of the Rebellion: A Compilation of the Official Records of the Union and Confederate Armies* (Washington, D.C.: U.S. Government Printing Office, 1880–1901), vol. 16, pt. 1, 1115 (hereinafter cited as *OR*. Unless noted, all references refer to Series I); Frierson quote from *OR*, vol. 16, pt. 1, 1118.

8. *OR*, vol. 16, pt. 1, 1114, 1116; Evan D. Davis speech manuscript, Libraries and Learning Resources, University of Wisconsin, Oshkosh; Marcus B. Toney, *The Privations of a Private* (Nashville, TN, 1905): 43–44; Hambleton Tapp, ed., "The Battle of Perryville, October 8, 1862, as Described in the Diary of Captain Robert B. Taylor," *Register of the Kentucky Historical Society* 60 (October 1962): 276; Sam R. Watkins, *Co. Aytch* (Wilmington, NC: Broadfoot Publishing Co., 1990 [1881–1882]), 83.

9. For further information about Cheatham's attack, see *OR*, vol. 16, pt. 1, 1113–19; Christopher Losson, *Tennessee's Forgotten Warriors: Frank Cheatham and His Confederate Division* (Knoxville: University of Tennessee Press, 1989), 66–73; Stuart W. Sanders, "All Did Their Duty Nobly Well," *America's Civil War* (November 2004): 22–28, 73; Stuart W. Sanders, "Perryville's Bloody Cornfield," *America's Civil War* (September 2002): 30–36, 64.

10. Robert S. Cameron, *Staff Ride Handbook for the Battle of Perryville, 8 October 1862* (Fort Leavenworth, KS: Combat Studies Institute Press, 2005), 158; *OR*, vol. 16, pt. 1, 1056; Noe, *Perryville*, 216–17. Twelve guns were initially on this ridge, but Captain Cyrus Loomis's battery had withdrawn by the time the Confederates attacked.

11. "The air" quote from John Beatty, *The Citizen-Soldier: The Memoirs of a Volunteer* (Lincoln: University of Nebraska Press, 1998 [1879]), 178; Alf Burnett, *Humorous, Pathetic, and Descriptive Incidents of the War* (Cincinnati, OH: R.W. Carroll & Co., 1864), 16. For information about the fighting on the Union right flank, see Stuart W. Sanders, "Buckeye Warriors at Perryville," *America's Civil War* (January 2001): 38–44, 86; and Kirk C. Jenkins, *The Battle Rages Higher: The Union's Fifteenth Kentucky Infantry* (Lexington: University Press of Kentucky, 2003), 66–81.

12. Noe, *Perryville*, 265; *OR*, vol. 16, pt. 1, 1123; Jenkins, *Battle Rages Higher*, 75; "brass bands" quoted in Kenneth A. Hafendorfer, *Perryville: Battle for Kentucky* (Louisville, KY: KH Press, 1991), 229.

13. Cameron, *Staff Ride Handbook*, 177; *OR*, vol. 16, pt. 1, 1123.

14. *OR*, vol. 16, pt. 1, 1025; Jenkins, *Battle Rages Higher*, 77; Noe, *Perryville*, 215; Cameron, *Staff Ride Handbook*, 114.
15. Kurt Holman, Perryville Order of Battle, Perryville Battlefield State Historic Site, Perryville, KY; *OR*, vol. 16, pt. 1, 1079; William Cunningham Letter, 59th Illinois Infantry File, Perryville Battlefield State Historic Site, Perryville, KY; Stuart W. Sanders, "Every Mother's Son of Them Are Yankees," *Civil War Times Illustrated* (October 1999): 56.
16. *OR*, vol. 16, pt. 1, 1159, 1111; Sanders, "Every Mother's Son," 57.
17. For information about Union and Confederate casualties, see Noe, *Perryville*, 369–80.
18. Edwin C. Bearss, "General Bragg Abandons Kentucky," *Register of the Kentucky Historical Society* 59 (July 1961): 271; Lowell H. Harrison, *The Civil War in Kentucky* (Lexington: University Press of Kentucky, 1975), 57.

CHAPTER 2

19. Watkins, *Co. Aytch*, 81.
20. *OR*, vol. 16, pt. 1, 1038, 1042, 1087; "Dear Amanda" letter, October 12, 1862, George W. Landrum Letters, Ohio Historical Society, Columbus, OH; Edgar L. McCormick and Gary A. DuBro, eds., "If I Live to Get Home: The Civil War Letters of Private Jonathan McElderry," *Serif* 3 (March 1966): 23.
21. Noe, *Perryville*, 369, 370, 372, 374. William T. Clark of the 79th Pennsylvania wrote that the largest number of dead and wounded could be found on the Union left flank. William G. Davis and Janet B. Davis, eds., *William T. Clark's Diary* (Lancaster, PA: Lancaster County Historical Society, 1989), October 8, 1862 entry. Regiments with casualty rates near 50 percent were more than likely engaged on the Union left. However, high casualty percentages were not confined to the northern end of the field. The 3rd Florida Infantry lost 41 percent casualties, the 33rd Alabama suffered 44 percent, the 10th Wisconsin lost 40 percent, the 42nd Indiana suffered nearly 36 percent and the 15th Kentucky lost nearly 40 percent. Noe, *Perryville*, 371, 372, 373. Casualties also listed in Kurt Holman, ed., Perryville Regimental Database File, Perryville Battlefield State Historic Site. Despite these high percentages, George Landrum of the 2nd Ohio wrote with disbelief, "It is perfectly astonishing that more were not killed. I have seen men fall all around, and others step into their tracks. I have

seen men shot in the head, breast, and legs, and still stand up and fire till they dropped down either dead or exhausted." "Dear Amanda," October 12, 1862, Landrum Letters, Ohio Historical Society.

22. See Surgeon General Joseph K. Barnes, ed., *The Medical and Surgical History of the War of the Rebellion* (Wilmington, NC: Broadfoot Publishing, 1990), 2: 255. For casualty statistics from the major engagements, see Grady McWhiney and Perry D. Jamieson, *Attack and Die: Civil War Military Tactics and the Southern Heritage* (Tuscaloosa: University of Alabama Press, 1982), 7.

23. Tarawa casualty statistics from James Bradley with Ron Powers, *Flags of Our Fathers* (New York: Bantam Books, 2001), 147; Normandy casualty statistics from *Army Historical Series: American Military History* (Washington, D.C.: Center of Military History, United States Army, 1989), 487.

24. Holman, Regimental Database File.

25. Noe, *Perryville*, 371; *Atlanta Southern Confederacy*, November 12, 1862.

26. Tapp, "Diary of Captain Robert B. Taylor," 280; United States Sanitary Commission, *Report No. 55, Operations of the Sanitary Commission at Perryville, KY* (Louisville, KY: U.S. Sanitary Commission, 1862), 8; Barnes, *Medical and Surgical History*, 2: 255.

27. McDonough, *War in Kentucky*, 303; John Henry Otto, *War Memories* (transcript of memoirs in 21st Wisconsin Infantry File, Perryville Battlefield State Historic Site, Perryville, KY), 100. Casualty statistics from Noe, *Perryville*, 374. The 645 men of the 105th Ohio lost 51 killed, 147 wounded and 6 missing.

28. "My War Record" (anonymous memoirs of service in the 41st Georgia Infantry File, Perryville Battlefield State Historic Site, Perryville, KY).

29. Otto, *War Memories*, 99–102.

30. Walter Jeffers Vaughan, "The Brand of Coward: Masculine and Patriotic Expectations in a Civil War Town" (PhD diss., Case Western Reserve University, 1996), 289. Copy on file at the Perryville Battlefield Preservation Association, Perryville, KY. While most members of the 41st Georgia were raw troops, some soldiers had seen combat in other regiments prior to Perryville. Other Pennsylvanians were wounded by buck and ball rounds, including William T. Clark of Company B, 79th Pennsylvania, who was "wounded in the side flesh wound, buck shot between the elbow & one near the right shoulder." Davis and Davis, *William T. Clark's Diary*, October 8, 1862 entry.

31. "Almost under the brass guns…" *Confederate Veteran* 17 (April 1909): 163; "Captain 'Dick' Steele," *Confederate Veteran* 19 (August 1911): 393.

32. Capt. W.W. Carnes, "Artillery at the Battle of Perryville," *Confederate Veteran* 33 (January 1925): 9; B.F. Cheatham, "The Battle of Perryville," *Southern Bivouac* 4 (April 1886): 705.

33. Peter Cozzens, ed., "Ambition Carries the Day: William Passmore Carlin Recalls the Battle of Perryville, Kentucky," *Columbiad* 1 (Spring 1997): 146; William H. Ball, "At Perryville," *National Tribune* (December 15, 1887), 2; *National Republican* [Washington, D.C.], October 20, 1862. The correspondent probably walked along the Chaplin River to the Goodnight farm from the Crawford Spring, a fairly direct route. The Crawford House, located above the spring and on the Harrodsburg Road, was Bragg's headquarters during the battle.

34. Davis Biggs, "Incidents in the Battle of Perryville, Ky.," *Confederate Veteran* 33 (April 1925): 142; *Cincinnati Daily Enquirer*, October 17, 1862. For Confederates stripping Northern dead, see also "Dear Amanda," October 12, 1862, Landrum Letters, Ohio Historical Society; and Robert J. Winn Diary, Ohio Historical Society.

35. George Morgan Kirkpatrick, *The Experiences of a Private Soldier of the Civil War* (Indianapolis, IN: Hoosier Bookshop, 1973), 15, 17; *Report of the Adjutant General of the State of Indiana* (Indianapolis, IN: W.R. Holloway, State Printer, 1865), 2: 413; S.F. Horrall, *History of the Forty-Second Indiana Volunteer Infantry* (n.p., 1892), 152; James Maynard Shanklin, *"Dearest Lizzie": The Civil War as Seen Through the Eyes of Lieutenant Colonel James Maynard Shanklin of Southwest Indiana's Own 42nd Indiana Regiment, Indiana Volunteer Infantry* (Evansville, IN: Friends of Williard Library Press, 1988), 234.

36. Williamson quoted in McDonough, *War in Kentucky*, 290. A trooper in John Wharton's Rebel cavalry also endured the cries of the injured. "No man ever experienced such a night of torture as we did listening to our wounded comrades, prostrate on the hot earth, crying for water," he wrote. "The litter corps worked without cessation throughout the night conveying the wounded off the field." W.H. Davis, "Recollections of Perryville," *Confederate Veteran* 20 (May 1912): 554.

37. Elizabeth E.P. Bascom, ed., "'Dear Lizzie': Letters Written by James 'Jimmy' Garvin Crawford to his Sweetheart Martha Elizabeth 'Lizzie' Wilson while He Was in the Federal Army During the War Between the States, 1862–1865" (photocopy of transcribed letters in the 80th Illinois Infantry File, Perryville Battlefield State Historic Site, Perryville, KY), 35.

38. Mead Holmes Sr., ed., *A Soldier of the Cumberland: Memoir of Mead Holmes, Jr.* (Boston: American Tract Society, 1864), 94–95.

CHAPTER 3

39. L.G. Bennett and William M. Haigh, *History of the Thirty-Sixth Regiment Illinois Volunteers* (Aurora, IL: Knickerbocker and Hodder, 1876), 275; Hoosier quote from Lieut. R.V. Marshall, *An Historical Sketch of the Twenty-Second Regiment, Indiana Volunteers* (Madison, IN: Courier Co., 1884), 24.

40. Samuel M. Starling, "Dearest Daughters" letter, November 16, 1862, Lewis-Starling Manuscript Collection, Western Kentucky University.

41. *Louisville Journal*, October 14, 1862. Maney's adjutant, Thomas Malone, saw a similar scene during a nighttime visit to the battlefield. He wrote, "I remember seeing what appeared to me to be a great bundle of rags, and Emmett Cockrill and I got down to examine it. It proved to be a body in which, it seemed, a shell had exploded, leaving no trace of humanity except blood and bones and shattered flesh." Thomas H. Malone, *Memoir of Thomas H. Malone* (Nashville, TN, 1928), 133.

42. After his Perryville experiences, McChord suffered nightmares for weeks. He wrote that whenever he shut his eyes, he could "see thousands of glaring eyes staring at me from all sides," which made him "wake with a start." He added that because of his battlefield memories, "it was many days before I could regain my normal condition." William Caldwell McChord, "Memoirs of William Caldwell McChord" (transcript of unpublished memoirs in Perryville Battlefield Preservation Association files, Perryville, KY), 36–37.

43. Christen Ashby Cheek, ed., "Memoirs of Mrs. E.B. Patterson: A Perspective on Danville During the Civil War," *Register of the Kentucky Historical Society* 92 (Autumn 1994): 384–85.

44. Thomas P. Davis, *"Time Wears Wearily On": An Unromantic Picture of the Civil War* (Jacksonville, FL: Historical Records Survey, WPA, ca. 1930), 4; Thomas T. Haver, ed., *Forty-Eight Days: The 105th Ohio Volunteer Infantry, Camp Cleveland, Ohio, to Perryville, Kentucky* (Amherst, MA: Collective Copies, 1997), 39.

45. Arnold Gates, ed., *The Rough Side of War: The Civil War Journal of Chesley A. Mosman, 1st Lieutenant, Co. D, 59th Illinois Volunteer Infantry Regiment* (Garden City, NY: Basin Publishing Company, 18978), 31; D. Lathrop, *The History of the Fifty-Ninth Regiment Illinois Volunteers* (Indianapolis, IN: Hall and Hutchinson, 1865), 169.

46. *OR*, vol. 16, pt. 1, 1080; Corporal George W. Herr, *Nine Campaigns in Nine States: The History of the Fifty-Ninth Regiment Illinois Veteran Volunteer Infantry* (San Francisco, CA: Bancroft Company, 1890), 117.

47. Jefferson J. Polk, *Autobiography of J.J. Polk* (Louisville, KY: John P. Morton and Co., 1867), 97.

48. George W. Landrum Letters, Ohio Historical Society, 93.

49. Eastham Tarrant, *Wild Riders of the First Kentucky Cavalry* (West Jefferson, OH: Genesis Publishing Co., 1997 [1894]), 167; Marianne C. Johnston, *The Young Chaplain* (New York: N. Tibbbals & Sons, Publishers, 1876), 103.

50. Union cavalryman quoted in Lewis Collins, *History of Kentucky* (Salem, MA: Higginson Book Company, 1874), 1: 114; "eaten by buzzards" quoted in Hafendorfer, *Perryville*, 423.

51. The story of a military execution on the field is corroborated by William T. Clark of the 79th Pennsylvania Infantry. Clark wrote, "In one pen of rails I saw 18 dead rebels, one of whom had not been shot more than 10 minutes. He was a Spy in our camp." Davis and Davis, *William T. Clark's Diary*, October 8, 1862 entry.

52. Artilleryman William Ball of the 5th Wisconsin Light Artillery also saw this "magnificent shot." He wrote, "I saw one soldier with his head blown off by a shell or cannon-ball, nothing being left but a portion of his lower jaw; another was literally cut in two by the same means." William H. Ball, "At Perryville: What An Artilleryman Saw of that Battle," *National Tribune* 7 (December 15, 1887): 1–2.

53. The story of the three officers' battlefield tour, the execution of the Confederate and the tale of the female soldier are from Chillion Hazzard, ed., "A Broken Link: A Story of the Battle of Perryville," *Monongahela* [PA] *Republican* 14 (January 12, 1865): 1. Transcript on file at the Perryville Battlefield Preservation Association, Perryville, KY.

54. Holmes, *A Soldier of the Cumberland*, 96–97; George W. Morris, *History of the Eighty-First Regiment of Indiana Volunteer Infantry* (Louisville, KY: Franklin, 1901), 18.

55. Henry Fales Perry, *History of the Thirty-Eighth Regiment, Indiana Volunteer Infantry* (Palo Alto, CA: F.A. Stuart, 1906), 37; Charles Lewis Francis, *Narrative of a Private Soldier* (Brooklyn, NY: William Jenkins and Company, 1879), 59. Many eyewitnesses commented on the piled fence rails or pens that were built to protect the bodies. Perryville Dr. Jefferson J. Polk also saw these pens, writing, "I saw dead rebels piled up in pens like hogs." Polk, *Autobiography*, 97. Two days after the battle, a member of the 5th Indiana Battery rode across the field and wrote, "The rebel dead were lying where they fell. [T]he slaughter was terrible, in some places the corpses had to be moved to let teams pass[. At] one place one rail pen had 11 dead men

in it...There were several such pens, their comrades had thrown them in the pens to keep the hogs [off of] them & had left in too big a hurry to bury." Daniel H. Chandler Collection, "History of the 5ᵗʰ Indiana Battery," Indiana State Library, Indianapolis, 25. Pennsylvanian William T. Clark recalled, "In one pen of rails I saw 18 dead rebels." Davis and Davis, *William T. Clark's Diary*, October 8, 1862 entry. After the August 1862 Battle of Richmond, Kentucky, hogs rooted up the bodies of buried Confederate soldiers. On October 24, 1862, the *Louisville Journal* reported, "Such of the hogs as are left between Richmond (Ky.) And Fort Big Hill are said to have been feasting lately upon dead rebels. We don't think we shall buy our winter's pork from that section." *Louisville Journal*, October 24, 1862.

56. "Most horrid sight," quoted in Grady McWhiney, *Braxton Bragg and Confederate Defeat* (Tuscaloosa: University of Alabama Press, 1969), 319; "now held possession" from Hazzard, "A Broken Link," 2; "in one place lay" from *New Albany Daily Ledger*, October 21, 1862. Holmes of the 21ˢᵗ Wisconsin helped with battlefield interments and commented on the animals. "It seems hard to throw men in all together and heap earth upon them, but it is far better than to have them lie moldering in the sun," he wrote. "Oh! to see the dead rebels in the woods...every where the eye rests on one, and this is not on the *field proper*...It is a fearful sight; and to think of all these soldiers having friends who would give any thing for their bloated, decaying bodies, now torn by swine and crows." Holmes, *A Soldier of the Cumberland*, 96.

57. Wilbur F. Hinman, *The Story of the Sherman Brigade* (Alliance, OH: Daily Review, 1897), 296.

Chapter 4

58. *Operations of the Sanitary Commission at Perryville*, 7.

59. Barnes, *Medical and Surgical History*, 2: 253; Davis and Davis, *William T. Clark's Diary*, October 8, 1862 entry.

60. Hinman, *Story of the Sherman Brigade*, 296. Few accounts mention the scores of horses that were slain during the Battle of Perryville. On the Union left flank, for example, at least thirty-five horses were killed on one narrow hill where twelve Federal cannon were posted. No known accounts mention what happened to the dead horses. It is likely that their carcasses were burned.

61. *Louisville Journal*, October 13, 1862; O.P. Cutter, *Our Battery, or the Journal of Company B, 1ˢᵗ O.V.A.* (Cleveland, OH: Nevins Book and Job Printing Establishment, 1864), 83. William Clark of the 79ᵗʰ Pennsylvania wrote, "Perryville is a fine little place but much scattered...All the large houses are occupied as hospitals for the wounded loyal & Secesh." He added, "The dead and dying are in every house." Davis and Davis, *William T. Clark's Diary*, October 8, 1862 entry. Union officer Nicholas L. Anderson of the 6ᵗʰ Ohio noted that the "houses [were] riddled." Isabel Anderson, ed., *The Letters and Journal of General Nicholas Longworth Anderson* (New York: Fleming H. Revell Co., 1942), 162.

62. Burnett, *Humorous, Pathetic, and Descriptive Incidents*, 14; *Operations of the Sanitary Commission at Perryville*, 10.

63. Kurt Holman, ed., Perryville Casualty Computer Database File, Perryville Battlefield State Historic Site, Perryville, KY.

64. L.W. Day, *Story of the One Hundred and First Ohio Infantry* (Cleveland, OH: W.M. Bayne Printing Co., 1894), 55.

65. Joan W. Albertson, ed., *Letters Home to Minnesota: 2ⁿᵈ Minnesota Volunteers* (Spokane, WA: P.D. Enterprises, 1992), letter no. 58, page 2.

66. Polk, *Autobiography*, 45; Jefferson J. Polk file, Perryville Battlefield Preservation Association, Perryville, KY; Mrs. S.J. Andrus [Sarah Coleman], "A War Incident," 10ᵗʰ Wisconsin Infantry File, Perryville Battlefield State Historic Site, Perryville, KY.

67. Andrus, "War Incident," 1, 3–4.

68. Ibid., 5–6.

69. Ibid., 6–7.

70. Ibid., 10–11.

71. Lora Parks, "The Karrick-Parks House," Karrick-Parks House File, Perryville Battlefield Preservation Association, Perryville, KY; Charles Kays, ed., Synopsis of John C. Russell War Claim, Russell House File, Perryville Battlefield Preservation Association, Perryville, KY. The original claim can be found at the National Archives, Washington, D.C., Record Group 92, Records of the Quartermaster General, Entry #817, File #217/1019.

72. S.K. Crawford, "Battle of Perryville: How It Looked to a Surgeon at the Rear of the Army," *National Tribune* 12 (April 2, 1893): 4; *Cincinnati Daily Enquirer*, October 17, 1862.

73. Otto, *War Memories*, 96.

74. *New Albany Daily Ledger*, October 21, 1862; Day, *Story of the One Hundred and First Ohio Infantry*, 55.

75. Polk, *Autobiography*, 98.

76. Holman, Perryville Casualty Database File; Adam S. Johnston, *The Soldier Boy's Diary Book* (Pittsburgh, PA: 1866), 23–25.

77. John L. Berkley, ed., *In Defense of the Flag: The Civil War Diary of Pvt. Ormond Hupp, 5ᵗʰ Indiana Light Artillery* (Freedonia, NY, 1992), 21.

78. Ibid., 21–22.

79. Ibid., 22.

80. Ibid., 22–23.

81. Ibid., 23.

82. Ibid., 23–24; *New Albany Daily Ledger*, October 20, 1862.

83. Berkley, *In Defense of the Flag*, 24–26.

84. Ibid., 22; Holman, Perryville Casualty Database File. P.M. Radford wrote that maintaining separate military cemeteries was expensive because "a house had to be built, lands fenced, and the salaries of a keeper and hands to keep the place in order [needed to be] paid." P.M. Radford, "Where Heroes Rest," *National Tribune* (November 1, 1883): 1.

CHAPTER 5

85. Cheatham, "The Battle of Perryville," 705.

86. Watkins, *Co. Aytch*, 83. In his memoir, Watkins mistakenly names Irwin as "Lute B. Irving."

87. "Dr. Lewis Broyles Irwin," *Confederate Veteran* 17 (November 1909): 565.

88. Watkins, *Co. Aytch*, 83; "Dr. Lewis Broyles Irwin," 565. Watkins and Marcus Toney of Company B, 1ˢᵗ Tennessee, were both surprised that the fifteen-year-old Billy Whitthorne, shot through the neck while charging Starkweather's men, survived. Toney expected to bury him that night, but they never found his body because the boy simply walked off the field. Whitthorne's combat experiences continued long past this childhood wound. He fought in the Spanish-American War and eventually became a major in the U.S. Army. See Toney, *Privations of a Private*, 46. Another amazing tale of survival was Captain Dick Steele, the twenty-six-year-old captain of Company A, 1ˢᵗ Tennessee. Like Whitthorne, Steele was severely wounded while charging Starkweather's position. Treated at the Goodnight farm by Toney, Steele never fully recovered. His obituary stated, "He never recovered fully from the wounds, but for nearly half a century suffered cheerfully." See "Capt.

'Dick' Steele," 393. Steele's wound also listed in Holman, Perryville Casualty Database File.

89. "First. Lieut. John H. Woldridge," *Confederate Veteran* 21 (October 1913): 503; "Judge Andrew Jackson Abernathy," *Confederate Veteran* 23 (December 1915): 560; "Mother to the First Tennessee Regiment," *Confederate Veteran* 34 (August 1926): 290.

90. Ethel Moore, "Reunion of Tennesseans," *Confederate Veteran* 6 (October 1898): 483; "First Lieut. John H. Woldridge," 503. Jacob Stark, a veteran of the 79th Pennsylvania, was another late casualty. Stark died in 1891, and his obituary proclaimed that "he was seriously wounded at the battle of Perryville, and carried a bullet in his body ever since, from which he suffered considerably, and finally led to his death. The bullet was taken from his body after he was dead." "Mustered Out," *National Tribune* (January 21, 1892): 6.

91. "Mother to the First," 290; W.W. Cunningham, "Mrs. Sullivan, Soldier and Nurse," *Confederate Veteran* 7 (March 1899): 101.

92. Toney, *Privations of a Private*, 46–47; Cunningham, "Mrs. Sullivan," 101.

93. Toney, *Privations of a Private*, 45; Erastus Winters, *In the 50th Ohio Serving Uncle Sam* (n.p., n.d.), 21; Davis, "Recollections of Perryville," 554; Evan D. Davis speech manuscript, University of Wisconsin, Oshkosh.

94. Toney, *Privations of a Private*, 44.

95. Ibid., 45; Holman, Perryville Casualty Database File.

96. Toney, *Privations of a Private*, 45. Quintard's wartime memory from Arthur Howard Noll, ed., *Doctor Quintard: Chaplain C.S.A.* (Sewanee, TN: University Press of Sewanee, Tennessee, 1905), 60.

97. Toney, *Privations of a Private*, 45.

98. Ibid., 44–46.

99. James R. Fleming, *Band of Brothers: Company C, 9th Tennessee Infantry* (Shippensburg, PA: White Mane Publishing Co., 1996), 35.

100. Ibid., 35, 37; "Mrs. Florence Goalder Faris," *Confederate Veteran* 32 (April 1924): 152. Hall noted that some of the wounded were nearly naked because their clothes were torn from their bodies while the surgeons probed for wounds and operated.

101. Fleming, *Band of Brothers*, 37. Mrs. Barbee, Joshua's wife, was a sister to Union Brigadier General Speed S. Fry, who reputedly killed Confederate General Felix Zollicoffer at the January 1862 Battle of Mill Springs, Kentucky. General Fry also led Union troops during the Perryville campaign. Barbee's home is now known as the Old Crow Inn.

102. Fleming, *Band of Brothers*, 38.
103. Ibid., 39–40. In the *OR*, Major George W. Kelsoe of the 9th Tennessee reported that Hall was mortally wounded. It is an error that has been recorded for posterity. See *OR*, vol. 16, pt. 1, 1116.
104. Ritchey notice, *Confederate Veteran* 8 (December 1900): 541.
105. Maria Evans Claiborne, "A Woman's Memories of the Sixties," *Confederate Veteran* 13 (February 1905): 64. For Mills, see Harold Edwards, "Benjamin Mills, Kentucky Gunmaker," *Muzzle Blasts* (November 1988): 4–10, 55. McDaniels's body was moved to Bowden, Georgia, in 1872. Holman, Perryville Casualty Database File.
106. Claiborne, "A Woman's Memories," 64.
107. Holman, Perryville Casualty Database File; "Judge John M. Taylor," *Confederate Veteran* 19 (May 1911): 236; "Robert T. Bond," *Confederate Veteran* 20 (October 1912): 488, 576.
108. Holman, Perryville Casualty Database File; Fleming, *Band of Brothers*, 35; Toney, *Privations of a Private*, 47; McDonough, *War in Kentucky*, 296; John A. Martin, *Military History of the Eighth Kansas Volunteer Infantry* (Leavenworth, KS: Daily Bulletin Steam Book and Job Printing House, 1869), 21; Hinman, *Story of the Sherman Brigade*, 296.
109. Fleming, *Band of Brothers*, 37; pension quoted in David Gambrel, "Last Confederate in Town: Daniel Smith Stayed after Battle of Perryville to Care for Dead and Wounded," *Kentucky Advocate* (October 8, 1995).

Chapter 6

110. E.L. Davison, *Autobiography of E.L. Davison* (1901): 46–47.
111. Duncan C. Milner, "A Human Document," *National Tribune* (September 27, 1906): 6.
112. From the description of the house, it is likely the Henry P. Bottom House, located at the Confederates' left flank. Robert L. Kimberly and Ephraim S. Holloway, *The Forty-First Ohio Veteran Volunteer Infantry in the War of the Rebellion, 1861–1865* (Cleveland, OH: W.R. Smeille, Printer and Publisher, 1897), 35.
113. Barnes, *Medical and Surgical History*, 2: 254. Civilians and soldiers also suffered from the drought. As one member of the 21st Wisconsin noted, "Water was the first article needed." The problem was, he added, "there was no water anywhere near there exept [*sic*] the small spring

at Perryville." Otto, *War Memories*, 97–98. Since he said it was a "small spring," Otto is probably referring to a spring located behind the Harriet Karrick residence (now known as the Karrick-Parks House), located on Buell Street in downtown Perryville). An exasperated J.W. Laybourn of the 3rd Ohio remembered the lack of water. "There was certainly none in [Doctor's Creek]," he wrote, "else, why should our boys the next day after the battle, go back ten miles to obtain water for the wounded?" He wrote that many wounded spent two to three days on the field without water. J.W. Laybourn, "The 3rd Ohio at Perryville," *National Tribune* (July 16, 1894): 3.

114. Loren J. Morse, ed., *Civil War Diaries and Letters of Bliss Morse* (Wagoner, OK, 1985), 31; Holman, Perryville Casualty Database File.

115. A.J. West, "The Great Battle of Perryville, Ky.," unidentified [possibly *Atlanta Reporter*] newspaper article, October 1892 (photocopy in 41st Georgia Infantry File, Perryville Battlefield State Historic Site, Perryville, KY); Henderson quoted in McDonough, *War in Kentucky*, 291–92.

116. Barnes, *Medical and Surgical History*, 2: 253; Diary of Captain John D. Inskeep, Ohio Historical Society; James A. Barnes, James R. Carnahan and Thomas H.B. McCain, *The Eighty-Sixth Regiment, Indiana Volunteer Infantry* (Crawfordsville, IN: Journal Company, 1895), 68; *New Albany Daily Ledger*, October 20, 1862.

117. Barnes, *Medical and Surgical History*, 2: 252; *Operations of the Sanitary Commission at Perryville*, 1, 6, 8.

118. Barnes, *Medical and Surgical History*, 2: 253, 255; *Operations of the Sanitary Commission at Perryville*, 5–6.

119. Barnes, *Medical and Surgical History*, 2: 252, 254, 255; *Operations of the Sanitary Commission at Perryville*, 5–6.

120. *Operations of the Sanitary Commission at Perryville*, 7.

121. Burnett, *Humorous, Pathetic, and Descriptive Incidents*, 18–19. The widow was probably the Widow Gibson, whose home was caught in the path of Confederate Brigadier General Daniel S. Donelson's brigade, which opened the Southern assault.

122. Karrick Family file, Perryville Battlefield Preservation Association, Perryville, KY.

123. Polk, *Autobiography*, 45.

124. *Trustees of the Christian Church of Perryville, Kentucky, v. the United States*, Congressional no. 12,977, National Archives Record Group 123, Records of the United States Court of Claims, National Archives, Washington,

D.C.; Karl Langenbecker file, Perryville Battlefield Preservation Association, Perryville, KY.

125. Mable Kirkland Bottom, *Charles Kirkland Family* (Harrodsburg, KY, 1980), 4–5.

126. Kurt Holman, Synopsis of Henry P. Bottom War Claim, Henry P. Bottom file, Perryville Battlefield Preservation Association, Perryville, KY; *R.B. Bottom, Executor of the Last Will and Testament of Henry P. Bottom, Deceased, v. the United States,* Congressional nos. 9877 and 2514 (consolidated), National Archives, Washington, D.C. [hereinafter cited as Bottom War Claim]; McChord Memoir, Perryville Battlefield Preservation Association, 34; Stuart W. Sanders, "Broken in Spirit," *Kentucky Humanities* 1 (2000): 20–25; A.J. Herald, "Terrible Sight at Perryville," *National Tribune* 23 (April 28, 1904): 10.

127. Crawford, "Battle of Perryville," 4; "Here we found" quoted in Sanders, "Broken in Spirit," 23. Bottom was evidently "very popular with the Federal officers" in the area, most of whom probably visited the house when it was a hospital. Abstract of Evidence on Merits, Bottom War Claim.

128. Morris, *Eighty-First Regiment of Indiana Volunteer Infantry,* 17–18.

129. Abstract of Evidence on Merits, Bottom War Claim.

130. Holman, Synopsis of H.P. Bottom War Claim; Abstract of Evidence on Merits, Bottom War Claim; Claimant's Request for Findings of Fact, Bottom War Claim; R.B. Bottom testimony, Bottom War Claim.

131. Abstract of Evidence on Merits, Bottom War Claim.

132. Preston Sleet and others saw Union troops burning rails and using hay for bedding. Many witnesses saw Northern soldiers killing hogs, cattle and sheep. Others saw sheep hides and hog carcasses in Federal camps. Mingo Peters, a slave in 1862, testified that Northerners killed all of Henry's cattle, "except [for] a few milk cows." Peters ate some of the beef because he had not eaten for three days. He also saw Union troops butcher hogs and sheep. Simon Rothschild, a soldier in the 11th Kentucky Cavalry who knew Bottom, saw Union soldiers kill hogs, sheep and cattle and take Henry's hay. All information from the Bottom War Claim.

133. Holman, H.P. Bottom War Claim Synopsis; Claimant's Request for Findings of Fact, Bottom War Claim; Abstract of Evidence on Merits, Bottom War Claim; receipt and agreement between attorney Charles C. Fox and R.B. Bottom, April 29, 1914, H.P. Bottom file, Perryville Battlefield Preservation Association, Perryville, KY. There are two

original dismissal dates because the claim, first presented on July 4, 1864, was initially divided into two parts: quartermaster stores and commissary stores. Defendant's Brief on Merits, Bottom War Claim. Jerry Wilkerson testified that Bottom was not "on friendly terms" with many who testified against him. Wilkerson and others noted that because of their animosity, the anti-Bottom faction could not truthfully judge Henry's loyalty. William May said that Bottom was a Unionist slave owner and his wife's family was opposed to slavery. Abstract of Evidence on Loyalty, Bottom War Claim. Bottom did oppose the Emancipation Proclamation. Brief on Loyalty, Bottom War Claim.

134. Abstract of Evidence on Merits, Bottom War Claim.

135. J.B. Bolling Testimony, Bottom War Claim.

CHAPTER 7

136. J. Winston Coleman Jr., *Historic Kentucky* (Lexington, KY: Henry Clay Press, 1968), 135. For a history of the school, see Stuart W. Sanders, "The Ewing Institute: Perryville's Noted Antebellum School," *Kentucky Ancestors* 45 (Autumn 2009).

137. Coleman, *Historic Kentucky*, 135.

138. W.H. Parks Testimony, *Trustees of the Ewing Institute of Perryville, Kentucky, v. the United States*, Congressional no. 12,976, National Archives Record Group 123, Records of the United States Court of Claims, National Archives, Washington, D.C. [hereinafter cited as Ewing Institute War Claim]; Ewing Institute students serenading Bragg from Noe, *Perryville*, 105, and Hafendorfer, *Perryville*, 76.

139. Sandifer testimony, Ewing Institute War Claim; W.H. Parks testimony, Ewing Institute War Claim; C.T. Armstrong testimony, Ewing Institute War Claim.

140. Sandifer testimony, W.H. Parks testimony and C.T. Armstrong testimony, Ewing Institute War Claim.

141. J.A. Carpenter testimony, Ewing Institute War Claim.

142. Gay Broyles tuition information, Ewing Institute File, Perryville Battlefield Preservation Association, Perryville, KY; Coleman, *Historic Kentucky*, 135.

143. Ewing Institute War Claim.

144. Ibid.

145. Ibid; *Paducah Evening Sun*, December 28, 1910.

146. "Ewing Institute," undated newspaper clipping, Ewing Institute File, Perryville Battlefield Preservation Association, Perryville, KY; "Ewing Institute: Interesting Exercises at the Perryville Institution of Learning," undated newspaper clipping, Ewing Institute File, Perryville Battlefield Preservation Association, Perryville, KY; *Kentucky Gazette* quoted in Coleman, *Historic Kentucky*, 135.

147. Coleman, *Historic Kentucky*, 135; *Louisville Courier-Journal*, April 7, 1929; "Ewing Institute," Kentucky Historic Resources Inventory, BO-P-24.

148. *Trustees of the Methodist Episcopal Church South of Perryville, Kentucky, v. the United States*, Congressional no. 13,012, National Archives Records Group 123, Records of the United States Court of Claims, National Archives, Washington, D.C.; *Session of the Presbyterian Church of Perryville, Kentucky, v. the United States*, Congressional no. 12,998, National Archives Records Group 123, Records of the United States Court of Claims, National Archives, Washington, D.C.; *Trustees of the Christian Church of Perryville, Kentucky, v. the United States*, Congressional no. 12,977, National Archives Records Group 123, Records of the United States Court of Claims, National Archives, Washington, D.C.

149. Bennett and Haigh, *History of the Thirty-Sixth Regiment Illinois Volunteers*, 277.

150. *Record of the Ninety-Fourth Regiment, Ohio Volunteer Infantry, in the War of the Rebellion* (Cincinnati: Ohio Valley Press, 1890), 23; Abraham V. Knapp Diaries, Wisconsin Historical Society, trans. Christopher L. Kolakowski, vol. 3, October 8, 1862 entry; Angus L. Waddle, *Three Years With the Armies of the Ohio and the Cumberland* (Chillicothe, OH: Scioto Gazette Book and Job Office, 1889), 38; "Names of Men Buried in a Corn Field Under a Walnut Tree," 38th Indiana burial map, Indiana State Archives, Indianapolis, IN; Perry, *History of the Thirty-Eighth*, 37.

151. Beatty, *The Citizen-Soldier*, 181.

152. A.M. Crary, *The A.M. Crary Memoirs and Memoranda* (Herrington, KS: Herrington Times Printers, 1915), 76; Marshall, *An Historical Sketch of the Twenty-Second Regiment*, 24.

153. Mitchell, Captain William S. Mitchell's letters, typescript at Perryville Battlefield State Historic Site, 18.

154. Lathrop, *History of the Fifty-Ninth Regiment Illinois Volunteers*, 170; Burnett, *Humorous, Pathetic, and Descriptive Incidents*, 16. One Indiana infantryman wrote, "The dead! [H]ow thick they lay...many of the rebel dead lay

on the field for days before they were buried." John D. Barnhart, "A Hoosier Invades the Confederacy," *Indiana Magazine of History* 39 (1943): 144–91. Several Union sources note that the Confederates stripped and plundered Federal dead, including Perry, *History of the Thirty-Eighth*, 37. George Landrum of the 2nd Ohio Infantry wrote, "The Rebels stripped [our] wounded. By the side of every one of our dead man you would see an old pair of shoes and a greasy, filthy pile of clothes" that the Confederates had swapped for Union uniforms. Landrum Letters, Ohio Historical Society, 93. Other sources specify that the "Texas Rangers" stripped the dead Federal troops. See Robert J. Winn Diary, Ohio Historical Society, Columbus, OH; and Frank M. Phelps letters, Book 14, Lewis Leight Jr., Collection, U.S. Army Military History Institute, Carlisle Barracks, PA.

155. *Operations of the Sanitary Commission at Perryville*, 9; McCormick and DuBro, "If I Live to Get Home," 24; Burnett, *Humorous, Pathetic, and Descriptive Incidents*, 16.

156. Beverly D. Williams testimony, Bottom War Claim; "Dear Amanda," October 12, 1862, Landrum Letters, Ohio Historical Society, Columbus, OH.

157. Holman, Synopsis of H.P. Bottom War Claim; Abstract of Evidence on Merits, Bottom War Claim; Otto, *War Memories*, 102.

158. Charles P. Fosdick, *Centennial History of the Kentucky School for the Deaf* (Danville: Kentucky Standard, 1923), 18.

CHAPTER 8

159. Holman, Perryville Casualty Database File. For information on the 33rd Alabama at Perryville, see L.B. Williams and W.E. Mathews Preston, eds., "The 33rd Alabama Regiment in the Civil War," Alabama Department of Archives and History, Montgomery, AL, 25; "33rd Alabama Infantry, Company B," 33rd Alabama Infantry File, Perryville Battlefield State Historic Site, Perryville, KY.

160. "Wheat straw" quote from Williams, "The 33rd Alabama," 27; "verey Dangerous" quote from G.D. Bush letter, October 22, 1862, 33rd Alabama Infantry File, Perryville Battlefield State Historic Site, Perryville, KY.

161. The story of Jesse is from Williams, "The 33rd Alabama," 28; Ward's burial listed in Boyle County Genealogical Association, *Boyle County*,

Kentucky, Cemetery Records, 1792–1992 (Utica, KY: McDowell Publications, 1992), 91.

162. Holman, Perryville Casualty Database File; R.S. Matthews, "Member of the Sixth and Ninth Tennessee," *Confederate Veteran* 20 (November 1912): 525. Confederate soldier Edwin Rennolds lamented that during the march back to Tennessee, "the ration was two biscuit[s] and two ounces of pickled pork, or three ounces of beef." Edwin H. Rennolds, *A History of the Henry County Commands* (Kennesaw, GA: Continental Book Co., 1961 [1904]), 49–50.

163. Casualty statistics and wound descriptions found in Kurt Holman, Perryville Casualty Database File.

164. J.M. Leonard to Mrs. J.C. Curtwright, October 27, 1862, photocopy of letter in 41ˢᵗ Georgia Infantry File, Perryville Battlefield State Historic Site, Perryville, KY. For information on the 41ˢᵗ Georgia at Perryville, see *OR*, vol. 16, pt. 1, 1113; and Sanders, "All Did Their Duty Nobly Well," 22–28, 73.

165. Curtwright burial information from "'Marse Jack' of the Troup Light Guard," Mary Evans Curtwright Collection, Troup County Archives, Troup County, GA.

166. Starling letter, Western Kentucky University.

167. Ibid. The party stopped at the Springfield home of E.L. Davison, who had gone to Centre College with James S. Jackson. Davison later wrote that "in the ambulance was my old College friend Gen. James S. Jackson…I stopped at the ambulance and looked at the coffin that contained my friend and thought of the happy days we had spent together. Now he was gone never to be seen again. This made me feel very sad." Davison, *Autobiography*, 49–50.

168. Starling letter, Western Kentucky University. Reverend Talbott, the former chaplain of the 15ᵗʰ Kentucky (Union) Infantry, conducted several military funerals after Perryville. Talbott gave eulogies for slain officers George Jouett and William Campbell of the 15ᵗʰ Kentucky and was also asked to perform the funeral for that regiment's colonel, Curran Pope, who died of typhoid fever after the battle. Talbott was recovering from dental surgery and was unable to preside over Pope's burial. Jenkins, *The Battle Rages Higher*, 81, 85. Jackson was reinterred in Hopkinsville on March 24, 1863. Thomas Speed, *The Union Regiments of Kentucky* (Louisville, KY: Courier-Journal Job Printing Company, 1897), 64; *The Biographical Encyclopaedia of Kentucky of the Dead and Living Men of the Nineteenth Century* (Cincinnati, OH: J.M. Armstrong and Company, 1878),

73; Ezra J. Warner, *Generals in Blue: Lives of the Union Commanders* (Baton Rouge: Louisiana State University Press, 1964), 248.

169. Hambleton Tapp, *The Confederate Invasion of Kentucky, 1862, and the Battle of Perryville, October 8, 1862* (n.p., 1962), 43n; Larry J. Daniel, *Soldiering in the Army of Tennessee* (Chapel Hill: University of North Carolina Press, 1991), 163; Losson, *Tennessee's Forgotten Warriors*, 73; McDonough, *War in Kentucky*, 295. For information about Bottom and the fight around his house, see Sanders, "Broken in Spirit," 20–25; and Sanders, "Buckeye Warriors at Perryville," 38–44, 86.

170. "Graves of Our Dead at Perryville," *Confederate Veteran* 3 (December 1895): 1; "An Article in the *Chronicle...*" *Confederate Veteran* 5 (December 1897): 620; Albert Kern, "Perryville Battlefield," *Confederate Veteran* 8 (August 1900): front cover.

CHAPTER 9

171. Estimates from Daniel, *Soldiering in the Army of Tennessee*, 71. In 1860, Harrodsburg had 1,668 residents, while Mercer County, of which Harrodsburg is the county seat, had 13,701 residents. Collins, *History of Kentucky*, 2: 265, 259.

172. Waddle, *Three Years*, 38.

173. Morris, *Eighty-First Regiment of Indiana Volunteer Infantry*, 18; Barnes, *Medical and Surgical History*, 2: 252.

174. Clark quoted in McDonough, *War in Kentucky*, 291; Holman, Perryville Casualty Database File.

175. Maria T. Daviess, *History of Mercer and Boyle Counties* (Harrodsburg, KY: Harrodsburg Herald, 1924), 106–7.

176. Ibid., 106; *Operations of the Sanitary Commission at Perryville*, 12.

177. Mary Hunt Afflick, "Southern Aid Society, Harrodsburg, 1861–5," *Confederate Veteran* 21 (January 1913): 30. In June 1865, members of the society set aside a day to decorate the Confederate graves in Harrodsburg's Springhill Cemetery with flowers.

178. *Operations of the Sanitary Commission at Perryville*, 11–12.

179. Ibid., 12.

180. Ibid., 11.

181. "To Whom It May Concern," *Olde Town Ledger* [Harrodsburg Historical Society newsletter] 81 (November/December 2002): 7.

182. Susan Matarese and James C. Thomas, "Shaker Communities," in *The Kentucky Encyclopedia* (Lexington: University Press of Kentucky, 1992), 812–13; all quotes from Earl D. Wallace, *The Shakers and the Civil War Battle of Perryville* (Harrodsburg, KY: Pleasant Hill Press, 1976). Also see Thomas D. Clark, *Pleasant Hill in the Civil War* (Harrodsburg, KY: Pleasant Hill Press, 1972); and David Marsich, "'And Shall Thy Flowers Cease to Bloom?' The Shakers Struggle to Preserve Pleasant Hill, 1862–1910," *Register of the Kentucky Historical Society* 109 (Winter 2011): 3–11.

183. Holman, Perryville Casualty Database File.

184. The story about Polk placing a guard around the church is an oral tradition. Author's conversation with Helen Dedman, May 2005; stained-glass windows too dark from "St. Philips on National Historic List," undated newspaper clipping, Perryville Battlefield Preservation Association files, Perryville, KY.

185. Barnes, *Medical and Surgical History*, 2: 255; *Louisville Journal*, October 29, 1862; *New Albany Daily Ledger*, October 20, 1862. Upon witnessing wounded Confederates in Perryville, one correspondent wrote, "Their wounded, too, are severely wounded, and will die rapidly." Since the slightly wounded Rebels went to Harrodsburg, he only saw the grievously injured at the battlefield. *National Republican* [Washington, D.C.], October 20, 1862.

186. *New Albany Daily Ledger*, October 20, 1862; *Memphis Daily Appeal*, November 7, 1862.

187. "Dear Folks at home," Andrew Phillips Letter, October 19, 1862, Kentucky Historical Society, Frankfort, KY; Bainbridge, Ohio, 1860 U.S. Federal Census, accessed online from www.ancestry.com on January 1, 2008; Holman, Perryville Casualty Database File.

188. "Dear Folks at home," Andrew Phillips Letter, October 19, 1862, Kentucky Historical Society; Holman, Perryville Casualty Database File.

189. *Memphis Daily Appeal*, October 20, 1862.

190. *Washington County, Kentucky, Bicentennial History: 1792–1992* (Paducah, KY: Turner Publishing Company, 1991), 98; Holman, Perryville Casualty Database File; transcript of Weinman letter, Thomas Allen to Catherine Wright, November 12, 1862, 21st Wisconsin Infantry File, Perryville Battlefield State Historic Site.

191. Winters, *In the 50th Ohio*, 23–24.

192. *Operations of the Sanitary Commission at Perryville*, 16, 17. For hospital trains after Perryville, see Ralph C. Gordon, "Hospital Trains of the Army of the Cumberland," *Tennessee Historical Quarterly* 51 (1992): 147–56.

193. *New York Times*, October 12, 1862; *Chicago Tribune*, October 10, 1862; Morgan A. Olson, trans., *Rollin Olson, 15ᵗʰ Regiment, Wisconsin Volunteer Infantry: Civil War Letters* (Minneapolis, MN, 1891), October 16, 1862 letter; "drank and quarreled" quoted in Dixie Hibbs, *Bardstown: Hospitality, History, and Bourbon* (Charleston, SC: Arcadia, 2002), 78–79.

194. Polk, *Autobiography*, 98; *Operations of the Sanitary Commission at Perryville*, 17; Holman, Perryville Casualty Database File.

195. S.K. Crawford, "Rear of Perryville," *National Tribune* 12 (June 8, 1893): 3

CHAPTER 10

196. Centre College Faculty Minutes, September 27, 1862, Centre College, Danville, KY. Centre College had several notable antebellum graduates, including U.S. Vice President John C. Breckinridge, who became a Confederate major general and the last Southern secretary of war. Other Confederate generals who graduated from the school included Thomas Hart Taylor, Joseph Horace Lewis, William T. Martin, Matthew D. Ector and Abraham Buford, who attended before transferring to West Point. Several notable Union officers also attended Centre, including Jeremiah Boyle, Speed Fry, T.T. Crittenden, James S. Jackson (killed at Perryville) and Union colonel and U.S. Supreme Court Justice John Marshall Harlan.

197. Cheek, "Memoirs of Mrs. E.B. Patterson," 371.

198. Barnes, *Medical and Surgical History*, 2: 252; Banks quoted in Emma Lou Thornbrough, *Indiana in the Civil War Era* (Indianapolis: Indiana Historical Bureau, 1965), 171–72.

199. Fanny Bell, "Dear Aunt Ann" letter, October 27, 1862, Perryville Battlefield Preservation Association Files, Perryville, KY.

200. *Operations of the Sanitary Commission at Perryville*, 9.

201. *Central University of Kentucky v. the United States*, Congressional no. 13,028, National Archives Record Group 123, Records of the United States Court of Claims, National Archives, Washington, D.C. [hereinafter cited as Centre College War Claim]; Stuart W. Sanders, "The Cost of War: Centre and the Battle of Perryville," *Centrepiece* (Fall/Winter 2003): 5–6.

202. Centre College War Claim; Sanders, "The Cost of War," 5–6.

203. Centre College War Claim; Sanders, "The Cost of War," 5–6.

204. *First Baptist Church of Danville, Kentucky, v. the United States*, Congressional no. 13,020, National Archives Record Group 123, Records of the

United States Court of Claims, National Archives, Washington, D.C. [hereinafter cited as Baptist War Claim]; *Operations of the Sanitary Commission at Perryville*, 14.

205. *Operations of the Sanitary Commission at Perryville*, 14.

206. *Vestry of the Trinity Protestant Episcopal Church of Danville, Kentucky, v. the United States*, Congressional no. 13,024, National Archives Record Group 123, Records of the United States Court of Claims, National Archives, Washington, D.C.

207. Baptist War Claim.

208. Ibid.; *Trustees of the First Presbyterian Church of Danville, Kentucky, v. the United States*, Congressional no. 13,066, National Archives Record Group 123, Records of the United States Court of Claims, National Archives, Washington, D.C. [hereinafter cited as Presbyterian War Claim].

209. *The Directors of the Presbyterian Theological Seminary of Danville, Kentucky, v. the United States*, Congressional no. 13,016, National Archives Record Group 123, Records of the United States Court of Claims, National Archives, Washington, D.C. [hereinafter cited as Seminary War Claim].

210. Ibid. The Danville seminary eventually merged with the Louisville Presbyterian Seminary. The main building deteriorated and was razed. In 1940, the site became Constitution Square State Historic Site.

211. Cheek, "Memoirs of Mrs. E.B. Patterson," 395; Stuart W. Sanders, "Civil War Soldiers Buried in Bellevue," *Kentucky Advocate* (October 6, 2002): D2. Two Union generals are also buried in Danville's Bellevue Cemetery: Jeremiah Tilford Boyle and Speed S. Fry.

212. *Operations of the Sanitary Commission at Perryville*, 14.

213. Bell letter, Perryville; Cheek, "Memoirs of Mrs. E.B. Patterson," 395.

214. Holman, Perryville Casualty Database File; Jenkins, *The Battle Rages Higher*, 400; Sanders, "Civil War Soldiers Buried," D2.

215. J. Stoddard Johnston, *Memorial History of Louisville from Its First Settlement to the Year 1896* (New York: American Biographical Publishing Company, 1896), 173; Collins, *History of Kentucky*, 1: 116; Jenkins, *The Battle Rages Higher*, 83, 84, 289, Sherman quoted, 85; W.H. Perrin, J.H. Battle and G.C. Kniffin, *Kentucky: A History of the State*, Edition 8-A (Louisville, KY: F.A. Battey and Company, 1888), 873, 874, Sherman quoted, 877; *Biographical Cyclopedia of the Commonwealth of Kentucky* (Chicago: John M. Gresham Company, 1896), 478; "fleshy part of my arm" from Pope's October 10, 1862 letter to the *Louisville Journal*, which was published on October 21. See also Pope's obituary

in the *Louisville Journal*, November 6, 1862; and Pope's obituary in the *Louisville Democrat*, November 6, 1862.

216. Cheek, "Memoirs of Mrs. E.B. Patterson," 397; Sanders, "Civil War Soldiers Buried," D2. Orcutt is buried in grave number 349 in the National Cemetery in Bellevue.

217. Centre College Faculty Minutes, May 27, 1863, Centre College, Danville, KY; Collins, *History of Kentucky*, 2: 87, 88; Sanders, "The Cost of War," 6. Green was born at Waveland, a stately home immediately south of Danville, in 1806. He graduated from Centre College in 1824. He became president of the college in 1858. That year, Centre student Walter Thwaites called Green "the prince of gentlemen." Walter Thwaites, "My Dear Sister" letter, November 23, 1858, Thwaites Family Papers, Kentucky Historical Society, Frankfort, KY. See also LeRoy J. Halsey, *Memoir of the Life and Character of Rev. Lewis Warner Green, D.D.* (New York: Charles Scribner and Co., 1871). Green is buried in Danville's Bellevue Cemetery.

218. "The Relief Corps," *National Tribune* (July 15, 1897): 6.

219. *Operations of the Sanitary Commission at Perryville*, 13n, 14.

220. Ibid., 9.

221. Fosdick, *Kentucky School for the Deaf*, 18.

222. Centre College Faculty Minutes, March 14, 1862, Centre College, Danville, KY.

CHAPTER 11

223. Many Kentucky Union soldiers were also angered over the Emancipation Proclamation. Although President Lincoln's edict did not legally affect Kentucky, pro-slavery Kentuckians believed that the Federal government could not legally interfere with slavery. While the colonel of the 8th Kentucky (Union) Infantry expressed dismay at the proclamation, most of the men in the regiment, who were recruited from eastern Kentucky, went AWOL for reasons other than the Emancipation Proclamation.

224. T.J. Wright, *History of the Eighth Regiment Kentucky Volunteer Infantry* (St. Joseph, MO: St. Joseph Steam Printing Co., 1880), 22, 48–51, 53, 55, 57, 60; Maude Barnes Miller, ed., *Dear Wife: Letters from a Union Colonel* (Ann Arbor, MI: Sheridan Books, 2001), 36, 39, 40, 42, 46–47.

225. Wright, *History of the Eighth Regiment*, 62, 63, 66–67, 68–69; Speed, *Union Regiments of Kentucky*, 348; Miller, *Dear Wife*, 54–55, 57.

226. Miller, *Dear Wife*, 55–56.

227. Ibid., 57; Wright, *History of the Eighth Regiment*, 69, 70; *Frankfort Daily Commonwealth*, December 10, 1862. For a statistical analysis of the AWOL soldiers, see Stuart W. Sanders, "Most Honorably Borne: Absences in the 8th Kentucky Union Infantry in 1862," *Kentucky Ancestors* 43 (Summer 2008): 172–82. For information on the flag raising, see Anthony P. Curtis and Kevin G. Smith, "Six Union Soldiers 'Planted Colors' on Lookout Mountain," *Kentucky Explorer* (March 2006): 58–60.

228. Lyman S. Widney, "From Louisville to the Sea," *National Tribune* (September 26, 1901): 7.

229. William L. Linney, "Perryville 50 Years Ago," transcription of ca. 1927 newspaper article in Perryville Battlefield Preservation Association files, Perryville, KY.

230. Calvin M. Fackler, *Historic Homes of Boyle County, Kentucky, and the Three Courthouses* (Danville, KY: Boyle County Historical Society, 1959), 4. Historian Richard C. Brown notes, "County officials lost use of their new courthouse for fifteen months." Richard C. Brown, *A History of Danville and Boyle County, Kentucky, 1774–1992* (Danville, KY: Bicentennial Books, 1992), 37.

231. Thomas A. Head, *Campaigns and Battles of the Sixteenth Regiment, Tennessee Volunteers, in the War Between the States* (Nashville, TN: Cumberland Presbyterian Printing House, 1885), 242.

232. Stewart B. Nixon, *Dan McCook's Regiment, 52nd O.V.I.* (n.p., 1900), 30.

A NOTE ON SOURCES

B ecause this book uses detailed endnotes, an exhaustive bibliography has not been included. Several key sources, however, have been essential. First, the backbone for this project has been the extensive research files located at the Perryville Battlefield State Historic Site. These files hold information about soldiers, civilians and institutions and include memoirs, diaries, regimental histories, maps, newspaper accounts, letters and more. In addition, computer database files pertaining to casualties and the regiments that fought at Perryville, compiled by Perryville Battlefield site manager Kurt Holman, have also been very useful.

For the Battle of Perryville, the essential source is volume 16 (parts 1 and 2) of the U.S. War Department's *The War of the Rebellion: A Compilation of the Official Records of the Union and Confederate Armies* (1880–1901). Kenneth W. Noe's *Perryville: This Grand Havoc of Battle* (Lexington: University Press of Kentucky, 2001) is also a comprehensive source about the battle, while James Lee McDonough's *War in Kentucky: From Shiloh to Perryville* (Knoxville: University of Tennessee Press, 1994) well describes the 1862 Kentucky Campaign.

Multiple accounts by soldiers who were caregivers or patients have helped tell the story of the aftermath, including Sam Watkins's *Co. Aytch* (1900); Marcus Toney's *Privations of a Private* (1905); Arthur Howard Noll, ed., *Doctor Quintard: Chaplain C.S.A.* (1905); Adam S. Johnston's *The Soldier Boy's Diary Book* (1866); Mead Holmes Sr., ed., *A Soldier of the Cumberland: Memoir of Mead Holmes, Jr.* (1864); and Samuel M. Starling's "Dearest Daughters" letter, November 16, 1862 (Lewis-Starling Manuscript Collection, Western Kentucky University).

Surgeons' accounts and medical reports include Surgeon General Joseph K. Barnes, ed., *The Medical and Surgical History of the War of the Rebellion* (Wilmington, NC: Broadfoot Publishing, 1990); United States Sanitary Commission, *Report No. 55, Operations of the Sanitary Commission at Perryville, KY* (Louisville, KY: U.S. Sanitary Commission, 1862); and Jefferson J. Polk, *Autobiography of J.J. Polk* (Louisville, KY: John P. Morton and Co., 1867).

Civilians' memories about the aftermath include Christen Ashby Cheek, ed., "Memoirs of Mrs. E.B. Patterson: A Perspective on Danville During the Civil War," *Register of the Kentucky Historical Society* 92 (Autumn 1994); William Caldwell McChord, "Memoirs of William Caldwell McChord" (transcript of unpublished memoirs in Perryville Battlefield Preservation Association files, Perryville, KY); E.L. Davison, *Autobiography of E.L. Davison* (1901); Alf Burnett, *Humorous, Pathetic, and Descriptive Incidents of the War* (1864); and Fanny Bell, "Dear Aunt Ann" letter, October 27, 1862 (Perryville Battlefield Preservation Association Files, Perryville, KY).

The best sources for information about institutions affected by the aftermath are war claims found in the National Archives in Washington, D.C. The endnotes list the various claims used for this book, but they include the claims of John C. Russell, Henry P. Bottom, Centre College, the Danville Presbyterian Theological Seminary, the Ewing Institute and various churches in Perryville and Danville.

For additional sources, please consult the endnotes.

INDEX

INDEX

ABOUT THE AUTHOR

S tuart W. Sanders is former executive director of the Perryville Battlefield Preservation Association. In addition to contributing to the books *Kentuckians in Gray: Confederate Generals and Field Officers of the Bluegrass State*, *Confederate Generals in the Western Theater* (volumes II and III) and *Confederate Generals of the Trans-Mississippi* (volumes I and II, forthcoming), Sanders has written for *Civil War Times Illustrated, America's Civil War, Military History Quarterly, Hallowed Ground, Kentucky Humanities, The Journal of America's Military Past, Kentucky Ancestors, The Register of the Kentucky Historical Society, Blue and Gray, Encyclopedia Virginia* and several other publications. He is currently a public history administrator in the Commonwealth of Kentucky.

Visit us at
www.historypress.net

CPSIA information can be obtained
at www.ICGtesting.com
Printed in the USA
LVHW080906170922
728617LV00003B/14

9 781540 206879